S0-BSF-322

3 0301 00088799 8

A BOOK OF AUSTRALIAN
VERSE

A Book of
Australian Verse

Selected and with an Introduction by
JUDITH WRIGHT

Geoffrey Cumberlege
OXFORD UNIVERSITY PRESS
LONDON MELBOURNE
1956

LIBRARY
College of St. Francis
JOLIET, ILL.

Oxford University Press, Amen House, London E.C.4

GLASGOW NEW YORK TORONTO MELBOURNE WELLINGTON
BOMBAY CALCUTTA MADRAS KARACHI CAPE TOWN IBADAN

Geoffrey Cumberlege, Publisher to the University

PRINTED IN GREAT BRITAIN

821.082

W 921

128,423

CONTENTS

v

CONTENTS

CONTENTS

CONTENTS

CONTENTS

CONTENTS

CONTENTS

CONTENTS

ACKNOWLEDGEMENTS

Acknowledgements and thanks are due to all the living poets, to publishers, periodicals, and other copyright holders, for permission to use the poems included in this anthology. A complete list is given below. Special thanks are due to the editors of the *Bulletin* and *Meanjin* and to Messrs Angus & Robertson for their assistance in tracing copyright holders.

Miss Ethel Anderson for 'Migrants'. Messrs Angus & Robertson for 'Where the Dead Men Lie' by Barcroft Henry Boake; 'We Woke Together', 'Sweet Silence after Bells', 'My Heart was Wandering', 'Let us Go Down', 'The Years that Go to Make Me Man', 'What Do I Know?', 'How Old is My Heart?', 'O Desolate Eves', and 'I Said, This Misery Must End' by Christopher Brennan; 'A Dream', 'Independence', 'Passivity', 'Lovers', 'Unit' and 'Adventure' by Mary Fullerton; 'The Roaring Days' by Henry Lawson; 'Colombine', 'June Morning', 'Enigma', 'Song of the Rain', 'Ambuscade', 'Morning', 'The End of Desire' and 'Fragment' by Hugh McCrae; 'The Fisher' by Roderic Quinn; 'Twelve O'Clock Boat' by J. A. R. McKellar. Mr Ken Barratt for 'Burke and Wills'. The *Bulletin* and Mr John Blight for 'Becalmed', 'The Cat-o'-Nine-Tails', 'Crab', and 'Stonefish and Starfish'. Mr Francis Brabazon for 'Victoria Market'. Mr Vincent Buckley for 'Korea'. The *Bulletin* for 'I Breathed into the Ash' and 'The Rock-lily's Pale Spray' by Roland Robinson. Mr David Campbell for 'Night Sowing', 'Heart of Light', 'The Monaro' and 'Beach Queen'. Messrs Chatto and Windus and Mr David Campbell for 'Men in Green' and 'Soldier's Song'. Mr C. B. Christesen for 'To the Rosella in the Poinsettia Tree', 'Do You Not Hear?' and 'Finale' by James Picot. Mr James Devaney for 'Mortality' and 'Winter Westerlies'. Miss Rosemary Dobson for 'The Missal', 'In My End is My Beginning', 'The Devil and the Angel (1)', and 'The Devil and the Angel (6)'. Mr Max Dunn for 'Flower of Exile' and 'I Danced Before I Had Two Feet'. Mr Geoffrey Dutton for 'A Prisoner Freed' and 'Nightflight and Sunrise'. *Meanjin* and Miss Patricia Excell for 'Forgotten Objects on a Beach'. The *Bulletin* and Miss Mary Finnin for 'Sarah Lorton' and 'Three Trees at Solstice'. Mr R. D. Fitzgerald for 'The cock that crowed this dawn up', 'Essay on Memory', '1918–1941', 'The Face of the Waters' and 'Traditional Tune'. Mr Leon Gellert for 'Before Action', 'In the Trench' and 'These Men'. Messrs Angus & Robertson and Dame Mary Gilmore for 'Dedicatory', 'Of Wonder', 'Boolee, the Bringer of Life', 'The Myall in Prison', 'The Waradgery Tribe', 'The Baying Hounds', 'Nationality', 'The Dice were Loaded' and 'The Tenancy'. Mr Max Harris for 'Lullaby', 'The Plowman', and 'Martin Buber in the Pub'. Mr William Hart-Smith for 'When You Touch', 'Drama', 'Baiamai's Never-failing Stream', 'Columbus Goes West', and 'Bathymeter'. Mr John Henderson for 'Of Love and Time'. Professor A. D. Hope for 'Australia' and 'Standardization'. Mr Peter Hopegood for 'Free Martin' and 'Dithyramb in Retrospect'. Mr Edgar Holt for 'Two Sonnets from a Sequence'. Mr

ACKNOWLEDGEMENTS

Rex Ingamells for 'Sea-chronicles'. Mr Eric Irvin for 'Midnight Patrol', 'Brother Ass', and 'Christmas 1942'. Miss Nancy Keesing for 'Old Men'. The *Bulletin* and Miss Eve Langley for 'Australia', 'Native-Born', and 'This Year, Before it Ends'. Mr Daryl Lindsay as trustee of the late William Dyson's estate for 'Death is but Death'. The Lothian Publishing Co. for 'The Crazy World' by William Gay; selections from 'The Gully', selections from 'To God: From the Warring Nations', and 'The Victoria Markets Recollected in Tranquillity' by Furnley Maurice; 'Song be Delicate', 'To a Blue Flower', 'Break of Day', ''Tis the White Plum Tree', 'The Orange Tree', 'Stony Town', 'Schoolgirls Hastening', and 'I Spoke to the Violet' by John Shaw Neilson; 'Love and Sacrifice' by Bernard O'Dowd. Mr J. P. McAuley for 'Blue Horses', 'New Guinea Lament', 'Missa Papae Marcelli' and 'The Death of Chiron'. Mr Ronald McCuaig for 'Betty by the Sea', 'Love Me and Never Leave Me', 'Is Love Not Everlasting?' and 'The Daily Round'. Miss Nan McDonald for 'Wet Summer: Botanic Gardens'. The *Bulletin* and Mr Kenneth Mackenzie for 'Caesura' and 'Confession'. Messrs Angus & Robertson and Mr Kenneth Mackenzie for 'Legerdemain'. F. W. Cheshire and Mr Kenneth Mackenzie for 'The Snake'. Messrs Dennis Dobson Ltd and Mr J. S. Manifold for 'Fife Tune', 'Suburban Lullaby' and 'The Tomb of Lt John Learmonth, A.I.F.' Mr Leonard Mann for 'The Earth' and 'Meditation in Winter'. Mr Ray Mathew for 'Young Man's Fancy', 'Let us not Pretend', 'Picnic' and 'The Poems come Easier'. Mr E. G. Moll for 'Beware the Cuckoo' and 'On Having Grown Old'. Georgian House and Mr Ian Mudie for 'Underground'. Mr Charles Osborne for 'So Fly by Night'. Mr John Philip for 'The Subject of the Bishop's Miracle'. Mr Hal Porter for 'Bi-focal'. Mr John Quinn for 'A Foxhole for the Night'. Mr Barrie Reid for 'St Kilda', and 'Nothing'. Miss Elizabeth Riddell for 'News of a Baby', 'Country Tune' and 'Forebears'. Mr Roland Robinson for 'Casuarina'. The *Bulletin* and Mr David Rowbotham for 'Little White Fox'. Lyre-bird Writers and Mr David Rowbotham for 'The Moment'. Mr Kenneth Slessor for 'Earth-Visitors', 'Stars', 'Five Visions of Captain Cook', 'Crow Country', 'Gulliver', 'Sleep', 'Five Bells' and 'Beach Burial'. The *Bulletin* and Mr Douglas Stewart for 'Old Iron', 'Terra Australis', 'The Sunflowers' and 'Helmet Orchid'. Mr Harold Stewart for 'Dialogue of the Way'. Mr John Thompson for 'Letter to a Friend'. The trustees of the Baylebridge estate and the Perpetual Trustee Co. of Sydney for 'The Ampler Circumscription', 'Sextains', and selections from 'Moreton Miles', 'Love Redeemed', 'A Wreath' and 'Life's Testament' by William Baylebridge. Mr Val Vallis for 'For This, the Tide'. Mr Brian Vrepont for 'Net-menders' and 'The Bomber'. Mr Francis Webb for 'The Gunner', 'For My Grandfather', 'Laid-Off', 'Morgan's Country' and 'Cartier at St Malo'. Miss Judith Wright for 'The Company of Lovers', 'Bullocky', 'Woman to Man', 'Woman's Song', 'Legend', 'The Ancestors' and 'To a Child'.

INTRODUCTION

Asked for an opinion on the question of 'who is the best of the moderns', Dylan Thomas once replied that the nice thing about poetry is that it isn't a competitive field. But the compiler of an anthology, however much he may agree with Thomas, is faced with the necessity of entering his poets in a kind of competition for space and attention, at least; and this lends itself to the notion that poets can in fact be graded according to quality, like apples or shoe-leather. But the anthology form, though it may be abused, has its uses also; and perhaps its chief justification, especially in so relatively small and recent a field as Australian poetry presents, is that it can act as a map does, showing the courses of rivers and the position of mountains, and giving, even in the debatable territory of immediately contemporary writing, at least some guide to possible routes of advance.

Australian writing, as such, suffers from the handicap of a brief and uncertain development, with its corollary of over-valuation in some directions, over-deprecation in others. It has not much more than a century and a half, in historical terms, to draw upon; much less in terms of self-awareness; and in so narrow a horizon, hillocks may look like mountains, while a real mountain might tower out of perspective too far for full appreciation. It is not much more than a generation since Furnley Maurice hopefully (and perhaps fallaciously) looked forward to the distant future when a great Australian poet might at last appear to build upon the foundations his predecessors had laid; and today, though there has been a great gain in self-confidence among the younger Australian writers, Maurice's rather anxiously apologetic attitude has not yet been outgrown. Nevertheless, there is, I think, a large enough body of Australian poetry, and enough writers of stature have contributed to its making, to provide a foothold on which some intelligent critical stance may be taken.

This anthology, therefore, is an attempt, not merely to gather together a few of the best Australian poems, nor to give a historico-national account of the development of Australian poetry which shall include selections from all those who have contributed to it; but rather an attempt to trace, however lightly, a sketch of Australian poetry up to the present day which shall yet be a selection of reasonably satisfying poems. I make this distinction because a good deal of Australian verse— particularly early Australian verse—while it has had its func- tion and importance in the growth of Australian consciousness, has little value beyond that function; its interest is historical rather than immediately poetic, a distinction unfortunately too seldom made by the more patriotic of Australian critics.

The difficulties of Australian poets have been many, and are still formidable enough. The most important has been the lack of any living link with the country itself. Australia was settled, in the first instance, by convicts and soldiery transported against their will, and in the second, by enterprising and materially-minded men anxious to make money and return to England as soon as possible. For many years a conception of Australia as a country to be loved or valued for itself was rare and difficult to uphold among such men and their descendants. What did arise among them was, not a love of the country as such, but rather of the freedom its great distances provided—a freedom from all that was implied by the convict system and by the colony's dependent status. Australia became a reality to its white settlers, in the first place, through the chance of political independence which it offered them, rather than through any deep emotional feeling for the land itself. Even

2

today, exploitation is the keynote of its economy, and respect for the soil and its natural growths of plant and animal, though it is increasing, is still painfully rare.

This forms no favourable climate for poetry, which needs a background in which emotional, as well as material, values are given their due weight; and the effect of this shallowness of roots is easily traceable in Australian writing, with its uneasy attempts to solve or to ignore the problem of its attitude to the country. Living in a land whose strange and haunting quality roused such a man as D. H. Lawrence, in his brief stay here, to write passages of splendid intuitive interpretation, Australian writers have found themselves without a true local idiom or feeling in their audience or themselves. This, perhaps more than any other factor, has turned Australian literature from the direction of interpretive, sensitive and experimental writing towards a more obvious and vigorous descriptiveness, in accord with the material 'tough-mindedness' of their culture.

The earliest writers to deserve the name of poet—Harpur, Kendall, a few others—left a surprising amount of work, much of it valuable in the attempt to develop a method of transmuting their unfamiliar surroundings into the forms of English verse, but little of any permanent poetic value. What they provided and, indeed, what they set out to provide, was a basis from which later poets might venture further into the unknown.

This basis was not, in any sense of the term, innovatory in technique or even in feeling. The problem, as these writers felt it to exist, was not that of adapting English verse-forms to the wholly new and strange country in which they found themselves, but, rather, that of forcing its essence into the forms already known to them—that of writing English verse about Australia. Traditionless they dared not be; they could not strip themselves of preconceptions and look at their new situation with new eyes, nor perhaps was it desirable that they should. The existing culture of the country—that of the aborigines—they felt to be so inferior as to warrant no examination. The blacks' mode of existence was to them not merely one of alien savagery, but of actual negation of the values of the civilization by which the white invaders lived—the values which formed their justification of that invasion. The aboriginal culture was based, apparently, not upon active mastery, but on passive acceptance of the environment—a static, Stone-Age adaptation (whose real riches in legend and in emotional interpretation of the country remained long unrecognized, and were in course of time largely lost as the aborigines disappeared before the white advance). Australian poetry, then, must be a re-affirmation of the English tradition; it must be English poetry written in the Antipodes.

Harpur, the first writer of importance, had one inestimable advantage over his nineteenth-century successors, in that he began to write early enough to be still under the influence of the early Romantics, in particular of Wordsworth. It is clear that the Wordsworthian attitude to nature would have been a tool of inestimable value in coming to terms early with the Australian scene, had it been used consistently and with intelligence. Harpur used it so in a few poems; it was a promising beginning.

But his immediate disciple and follower, Kendall, a generation younger than he, fell upon evil days. The later nineteenth-century debasement of the true romantic attitude had set in, in England; Wordsworth had given place to, at best, Tennyson, at worst, Tupper. Kendall had not the strength of vision nor the self-confidence which might have counteracted these weakening influences. His sensibility degenerated too often into sentimental over-sweetness; his lyricism became diffuse and flabby, his line loosened disastrously under Swinburne's later influence. He is represented here by the single sonnet in which he made a more honest judgement on his poetic—not his historic—achievement than has been made by many later critics anxious to inflate the work of Australian writers.

Adam Lindsay Gordon, Australia's most celebrated nineteenth-century writer of verse, though not himself Australian, has to his credit the establishment of the ballad-form in a state of respectability. Though the bush ballad, as such, pre-dated him by many years, and would no doubt have continued on its authentic rough-and-ready way without him, Gordon introduced it to the drawing-room. His own flamboyant latter-day Byronism was strengthened by its rougher rhythms, and he achieved a greater immediate popularity than any Australian poet has since enjoyed—with the possible exception of his follower in the tradition, A. B. Paterson ('The Banjo'). But Gordon, sentimental and swaggering, does not merit consideration among serious artists, though his work has its place in the honourable line of Australia's balladists, to whom an anthology might well be devoted.

The balladists—a group which includes, besides Paterson, Lawson and Brady, a number of lesser men down to the present day—did not contribute anything to the solution of the problems of Australian poetry, except incidentally in the emergence and solidifying in their work of an attitude to life which has come to be part of the Australian's idea of his own character—a kind of devil-may-care ironical swagger, self-conscious and adolescent enough, yet with elements of true masculinity. This attitude may be seen to colour the work of such writers as Slessor, Stewart, Campbell, Manifold, and even Fitzgerald. Manifold's poem *To the Tomb of Lt John Learmonth, A.I.F.*, is a conveniently obvious illustration of their influence.

The problem of Australian poetry, on the other hand, was accentuated after Kendall's failure to complete the work of

Harpur, by the *fin-de-siècle* self-questioning of Europe and England. Obvious cracks were beginning to appear in the tradition within which Harpur and Kendall had considered themselves as working; and, in addition, Australian national feeling was stirring in the movement which culminated in Federation in the early years of the twentieth century. The problem here resolved itself into two—the specifically poetic question of the relationship of Australian to English and European poetry, and the local problem of the expression of Australian national and environmental values.

The first was exemplified by the appearance of Australia's first poet of more than regional importance—Christopher Brennan.

Brennan, a scholar and an admirer of contemporary French poetry, in particular that of Mallarmé and his fellow-impressionists, brought to his writing a poetic sensitivity to rhythms and a sophistication of thought which Australian verse had never yet approached, and has seldom equalled since. The conflict which is the central source of his poetry is that of the individual in relation to his world and, further, to the universe: he sought to order his conception of life, so as to achieve the inner harmony for which he longed. Basically, then, his problem was that of the twentieth-century individual, whose values have dissolved in crisis. He is Australia's first truly 'modern' writer. It may be that the acuteness of the conflict in Brennan—so great as to end in personal tragedy—was accentuated by his lack of a critically informed audience and of a traditional background. His work has never been well known outside a small circle, and for many years after his death it remained out of print and practically unobtainable. The few lyrics given here cannot fitly represent his work, for his books were conceived as wholes, and should be read as such.

Brennan's contemporary, Bernard O'Dowd, attained a far

greater reputation in his day, but unlike Brennan's his work has dated badly. His early themes were those of the rational-Socialist group, sprung of the theories of Darwin, Bradlaugh, and the Fabian group in England, which enjoyed great popularity among the young intellectuals of the first years of the century. His verse, particularly his early verse, was often mere doggerel, and even his best work is marred almost beyond reading by vicious habits of cliché and ranting, and by a fustian manner in which useless allegorical abstractions strut in capital letters. But his nature was sincere and his idealism as genuine as it was naïf, and many critics can still be found to argue on his behalf as a poet. His reputation rests mainly on a long poem, *The Bush*, which attempts an ambitious and only half-humorous marriage between Greek historical and contemporary Australian themes. In a few stanzas, however, he reached in this poem a deeper level of understanding of the country and of the meaning of true patriotism than any Australian writer had done. Though it is copiously sprinkled with classical references, his work as a whole is that of a political patriot rather than of a scholar or poet in the true sense.

O'Dowd's popularity, and the success of *The Bush*, contrasted with the long neglect of Brennan, give a pointer to the later development of Australian poetry, which has been objectively, rather than subjectively, directed. Two notable figures, however, stand aside from this rule, though at opposite poles from each other.

The first, Shaw Neilson, was a born 'rhymer', a simple man whose art seems to owe nothing to study. A labourer for much of his life (he worked in quarries and as a road-maker until friends found him a less physically-exacting job in a city), and of little education and apparently little curiosity in the study of other poets' work, he composed 'in his head' and wherever the fancy took him, and much of his work was certainly lost for lack of opportunity to write it down. It is the lovely delicacy and sweetness of his best work—like the flavour of wild honey—which disarms one, striking the ear as strangely as a child's comment on the world. He has not the depth of feeling nor the observing eye of John Clare, to whom he has inevitably been compared: his quality is rather that of an untouched purity, of a spring-like vision as natural as the flowering of his own white Plum-Tree.

The second, William Baylebridge, is a writer of a very different order. He is philosopher as much as—at times more than—poet, and his recluse life and dedication to his work make him unique among Australian writers. Baylebridge's poetry has been called obscure, his philosophy dismissed as Nietzschean. Neither judgement is entirely true; for when his books are read as organic wholes, as he intended them, what seems difficult in the single poem becomes easy to interpret: and his philosophy owes more to Bergson than to Nietzsche, in its emphasis on the 'life-force', and in his treatment of time as that in which life constantly develops, evolves, and renews itself (a view which led him to a denial of the reality of death, birth, and creation, except as mere aspects of this constant onward surge). Yet there is much of Nietzsche in Baylebridge, and unfortunately it is at the point where Nietzsche fails both as philosopher and as personality that Baylebridge most resembles him.

Baylebridge's thought (which is often original and interesting, and which, as he himself insisted, is his own and not a mere derivation) led him to regard mankind as the crest of the forward movement of the life-force, and as embodying the hopes of God himself (in so far, that is, as Baylebridge acknowledged the existence of a God—a point on which he is occasionally self-contradictory). It follows that all must be subordinated to the fostering and development of those qualities in man (nobility, mental and spiritual adventurousness, selfless endeavour to increase the human heritage) which Baylebridge regards as forwarding the aims of the life-force. This comes close enough to Nietzsche's theories: and it is here that Nietzsche and Baylebridge slip into similar pitfalls. Both regard themselves as prophets of the future apotheosis of mankind, and this leads Baylebridge, as it had led Nietzsche, into a fatal inflation of thought, an unconscious elevation of himself to the position of arbiter of mankind's destiny. Baylebridge is quite in line with Nietzsche when he advocates eugenic improvement of the human race, and when he turns his attention to the modern development of nationalism; for he saw this upsurge of national feeling as the 'life-force' forging new tools for its own advancement, and his admiration for the qualities of leadership brought him to advocate something perilously close to totalitarianism. He recognized the dangers inherent in this, and the abuses to which it had in fact led, but did not cease to insist that these were avoidable excesses 'not fundamental to nationalism as a way of national life'. He regarded himself as the prophet of Australia's own rise to such a nationalism, and in the large volume *This Vital Flesh* he hoped to lay a philosophical, as well as a poetic, foundation for Australia's future contribution to the achievement of the human race.

This very brief glance at Baylebridge's considerable body of work should make it clear that he is not to be judged solely on his poetic merits. He aimed at very much more than that: in fact, it might be said that he looked on his verse rather as a vehicle for his theories than as an end in itself. 'Poetry exists to give shape and substance to the impulse that imagines (a reconstruction of the possibilities of this nature of ours)', he says in the preface to *This Vital Flesh*; and perhaps for this reason he seems to have made little attempt to evolve an individual mode of writing, but has rather modelled himself on earlier writers, especially Shakespeare and the seventeenth-century writers whom he admired, such as Donne and Carew. He is no mere imitator, however, for he uses his seventeenth-century mannerisms to clothe a thought in which he was himself passionately involved, and at his poetic best this leads to a fusion of style and emotion which can produce such poems as 'I worshipped, when my veins were fresh . . .'. His three best books—the sonnet-sequence *Love Redeemed*, the series entitled *Life's Testament*, and the later *Sextains*, perhaps his most characteristic production—make a formidable, and so far a much neglected, contribution to Australian literature.

Baylebridge is not likely to exert the influence on Australian life and character which he worked to achieve. His almost Germanic earnestness of purpose, his Nietzschean attitude to women, his advocacy of such unpopular causes as eugenics, his admiration for power, and its consequence in his leaning towards totalitarianism, are oddly out of place in the Australian climate of feeling. His is not an attractive poetic personality, but this should not lead to the neglect of his work, which at its best has a force and sinuosity of thought, an architectural strength, and a passionate sincerity which more than balance the inflated tortuousness of his unsuccessful verse.

The work of Hugh McCrae, influenced by Norman Lindsay and other members of Lindsay's immediate circle, represents a temporary reaction against the task of interpreting Australia, which had again been overtly taken up by Frank Wilmot ('Furnley Maurice'). Rather, McCrae in poetry, as Lindsay in his paintings, returned to the old Greek and Roman pantheisms for subjects. But these nymphs, centaurs, goddesses (not always convincingly re-imagined) achieved no real relationship with their new surroundings, and remain shapes of cardboard, as unconvincing against Australian backgrounds as, in O'Dowd's *The Bush*, contemporary Australian politicians and academicians look against their Greek background. McCrae's *The Ambuscade*, and a few other poems, however, attain a life of their own; and as a poet, McCrae reached at times a high level of technical assurance. Out of this period emerged Kenneth Slessor and Robert D. Fitzgerald, who, influenced by the Lindsay–McCrae group in their youth, have in their turn exerted a strong influence on the younger writers of the present day.

Slessor, whose *Five Visions of Captain Cook* is the progenitor of a great deal of verse, narrative and other, on the subject of the early voyagers of the Pacific, and whose terse, pictorial, image-laden style sets the tone of much recent writing, has written little since the publication of his selected volume *One Hundred Poems*. Fitzgerald, however, though his output is not really large, remains Australia's most influential poet. His best-known work, *Essay on Memory*, which won Australia's centenary prize for a long poem, did much to confirm the confidence of Australian poets in themselves; in spite of occasional unrewarding rhetoric and lack of incisiveness, it comes close to solving the difficulties inherent in the long 'philosophical' poem, and its wide sweep of thought and acceptance of large challenges was most heartening to those who hoped for the emergence of 'high' poetry in Australia. Fitzgerald has turned of late years to narrative poetry; his book-length poem *Between Two Tides* and the work of the younger poet Francis Webb and a few others have made for narrative poetry a place in modern Australian writing.

Over the years since the outbreak of war in 1939, a great deal of verse has been written and published in Australia. Because it is never possible to make final judgements on the course of contemporary and near-recent writing—a field in the course of almost daily change and re-balance—I have thought it best to give as broad an indication of the general shape and direction of the verse written in these years as seemed possible. Many of the writers represented are still young, and time will no doubt drastically alter perspectives in this latest portion of the anthology.

It only remains to mention that the anthology is arranged, in general, according to chronology of the writers' dates of birth. In a few cases I have set this aside to indicate that the period of a writer's important output has been later than that of his strict contemporaries—for example, in the case of Brian Vrepont, whose poetic output scarcely began until after his middle-age, and in the case of Mary Gilmore, who has been writing for many years, but whose later lyrics are upon the whole more successful than those in her early books.

It is only what actually happens in the development of a poetry, as of anything else, that has real interest and validity. The poetic theorizer is on dangerous ground when he points to any path as the true way for writers to follow. But I think it is true to say that, though her poets have served Australia well in the past, yet today, when Australia is assuming—or having thrust upon her—a far greater involvement in and responsibility for world events and world issues, few of her poets seem to be moving beyond the rather narrow limits of the tradition they have succeeded in establishing. Little poetry of importance has emerged over the years since the end of the war, and, of that, little has been preoccupied with questions of real moment. Yet, with the rest of the world, Australia faces an issue not merely strategic or political (with such questions of course poetry can have no concern, as poetry)—but basic to the human race; it is the issue of a choice between death and life. It seems time for the emergence in Australian poetry of some new impulse which may give it strength to deal poetically with this movement of a country from its position of shelter into the storm.

JUDITH WRIGHT

NORTH TAMBORINE
1955

CHARLES HARPUR

A Midsummer Noon in the Australian Forest

Not a sound disturbs the air,
There is quiet everywhere;
Over plains and over woods
What a mighty stillness broods!

All the birds and insects keep
Where the coolest shadows sleep;
Even the busy ants are found
Resting in their pebbled mound;
Even the locust clingeth now
Silent to the barky bough:
Over hills and over plains
Quiet, vast and slumbrous, reigns.

Only there's a drowsy humming
From yon warm lagoon slow coming:
'Tis the dragon-hornet—see!
All bedaubed resplendently,
Yellow on a tawny ground—
Each rich spot nor square nor round,
Rudely heart-shaped, as it were
The blurred and hasty impress there
Of a vermeil-crusted seal
Dusted o'er with golden meal.
Only there's a droning where
Yon bright beetle shines in air,

Tracks it in its gleaming flight
With a slanting beam of light,
Rising in the sunshine higher,
Till its shards flame out like fire.

Every other thing is still,
Save the ever-wakeful rill,
Whose cool murmur only throws
Cooler comfort round repose;
Or some ripple in the sea
Of leafy boughs, where, lazily,
Tired summer, in her bower
Turning with the noontide hour,
Heaves a slumbrous breath ere she
Once more slumbers peacefully.

O 'tis easeful here to lie
Hidden from noon's scorching eye,
In this grassy cool recess
Musing thus of quietness.

DANIEL HENRY DENIEHY

To His Wife

O pure of soul, and fond and deep of heart
    For those who darkened be,
Lift up thy holy voice at morn and eve
    And pray for me—

For me, who for this thronging world's hot strife
  A prize hath brought to be
Among the known—but sweet too dearly earned;
  Ah, pray for me.

Not aye the scholar's path a track of peace,
  Nor from the dread sins free;
Hard by the Isles of Truth doth Circe prowl;
  Oh, pray for me.

The spirit's hell-gloom and its hurricane
  Round studious cells may be;
Thou patient Moon of Memory's dreary sky,
  Oh, pray for me.

When through thy well-known window, oped beneath
  The uneasy, whispering tree,
Burn stars we children two have tried to count,
  Then pray for me.

At hour of rest, and when the moon makes pleased
  The melancholy sea,
And noon's surcease of happy household toil,
  Yes, pray for me.

Some solace for this wrung and rifted heart,
  That, wheresoe'er thou be,
Thou wilt, God's holiest gift, thou woman pure,
  Yet pray for me.

HENRY KENDALL

Prefatory Sonnet

I purposed once to take my pen and write,
    Not songs, like some, tormented and awry
    With passion, but a cunning harmony
Of words and music caught from glen and height,
And lucid colours born of woodland light
    And shining places where the sea-streams lie.
But this was when the heat of youth glowed white,
    And since I've put the faded purpose by.
I have no faultless fruits to offer you
    Who read this book; but certain syllables
    Herein are borrowed from unfooted dells
And secret hollows dear to noontide dew;
And these, at least, though far between and few,
    May catch the sense like subtle forest spells.

WILLIAM GAY

The Crazy World

The World did say to me,
    'My bread thou shalt not eat,
I have no place for thee
    In house nor field nor street.

'I have no land nor sea
    For thee, nor home nor bread;
I scarce can give to thee
    A grave when thou art dead.'

18

'O crazy World,' said I,
　'What is it thou canst give,
Which wanting, I must die,
　Or having, I shall live?

'When thou thy all hast spent,
　And all thy harvests cease,
I still have nutriment
　That groweth by decrease.

'Thy streets will pass away,
　Thy towers of steel be rust,
Thy heights to plains decay,
　Thyself be whirling dust;

'But I go ever on
I mount from prime to prime,
From an eternal throne
　I govern Chance and Time.

'Then, crazy World,' said I,
　'What is it thou canst give,
Which wanting, I must die,
　Or having, I shall live?'

BARCROFT HENRY BOAKE

Where the Dead Men Lie

Out on the wastes of the Never Never—
That's where the dead men lie!
There where the heat waves dance for ever—
That's where the dead men lie!

19

That's where the Earth's loved sons are keeping
Endless tryst: not the west wind sweeping
Feverish pinions can wake their sleeping—
Out where the dead men lie!

Where brown Summer and Death have mated—
That's where the dead men lie!
Loving with fiery lust unsated—
That's where the dead men lie!
Out where the grinning skulls bleach whitely
Under the saltbush sparkling brightly;
Out where the wild dogs chorus nightly—
That's where the dead men lie!

Deep in the yellow, flowing river—
That's where the dead men lie!
Under the banks where the shadows quiver—
That's where the dead men lie!
Where the platypus twists and doubles,
Leaving a train of tiny bubbles;
Rid at last of their earthly troubles—
That's where the dead men lie!

East and backward pale faces turning—
That's how the dead men lie!
Gaunt arms stretched with a voiceless yearning—
That's how the dead men lie!
Oft in the fragrant hush of nooning,
Hearing again their mothers' crooning,
Wrapt for aye in a dreamful swooning—
That's how the dead men lie!

Only the hand of Night can free them—
That's when the dead men fly!

Only the frightened cattle see them—
See the dead men go by!
Cloven hoofs beating out one measure,
Bidding the stockmen know no leisure—
That's when the dead men take their pleasure!
That's when the dead men fly!

Ask, too, the never-sleeping drover:
He sees the dead pass by;
Hearing them call to their friends—the plover,
Hearing the dead men cry;
Seeing their faces stealing, stealing,
Hearing their laughter pealing, pealing,
Watching their grey forms wheeling, wheeling
Round where the cattle lie!

Strangled by thirst and fierce privation—
That's how the dead men die!
Out on Moneygrub's farthest station—
That's how the dead men die!
Hard-faced greybeards, youngsters callow,
Some mounds cared for, some left fallow,
Some deep down, yet others shallow;
Some having but the sky.

Moneygrub, as he sips his claret,
Looks with complacent eye
Down at his watch-chain, eighteen-carat—
There, in his club, hard by
Recks not that every link is stamped with
Names of the men whose limbs are cramped with
Too long lying in grave-mould, camped with
Death where the dead men lie.

BERNARD O'DOWD

Love and Sacrifice

Can we not consecrate
  To man and God above
This volume of our great
  Supernal tide of love?

'Twere wrong its wealth to waste
  On merely me and you,
In selfish touch and taste
  As other lovers do.

This love is not as theirs:
  It came from the Divine,
Whose glory still it wears,
  And print of whose design.

The world is full of woe,
  The time is blurred with dust,
Illusions breed and grow,
  And eyes' and flesh's lust.

The mighty league with Wrong
  And stint the weakling's bread;
The very lords of song
  With Luxury have wed.

Fair Art deserts the mass,
  And loiters with the gay;
And only gods of brass
  Are popular today.

Two souls with love inspired,
　　Such lightning love as ours,
Could spread, if we desired,
　　Dismay among such powers.

Could social stables purge
　　Of filth where festers strife:
Through modern baseness surge
　　A holier tide of life.

Yea, two so steeped in love
　　From such a source, could draw
The angels from above
　　To lead all to their Law.

We have no right to seek
　　Repose in rosy bower,
When Hunger thins the cheek
　　Of childhood every hour:

Nor while the tiger, Sin,
　　'Mid youths and maidens roams,
Should Duty skulk within
　　These selfish cosy homes.

Our place is in the van
　　With those crusaders, who
Maintain the rights of man
　　'Gainst Despot and his crew.

If sacrifice may move
　　Their load of pain from men,
The greatest right of Love
　　Is to renounce It then.

Ah, Love, the earth is woe's,
   And sadly helpers needs:
And, till its burden goes,
   Our work is—where it bleeds.

HENRY LAWSON

The Roaring Days

The night too quickly passes
And we are growing old,
So let us fill our glasses
And toast the Days of Gold;
When finds of wondrous treasure
Set all the South ablaze,
And you and I were faithful mates
All through the roaring days!

Then stately ships came sailing
From every harbour's mouth,
And sought the Land of Promise
That beaconed in the South;
Then southward streamed their steamers
And swelled their canvas full
To speed the wildest dreamers
E'er borne in vessel's hull.

Their shining Eldorado
Beneath the southern skies
Was day and night for ever
Before their eager eyes.

The brooding bush, awakened,
Was stirred in wild unrest,
And all the year a human stream
Went pouring to the West.

The rough bush roads re-echoed
The bar-room's noisy din,
When troops of stalwart horsemen
Dismounted at the inn.
And oft the hearty greetings
And hearty clasp of hands
Would tell of sudden meetings
Of friends from other lands.

And when the cheery camp-fire
Explored the bush with gleams,
The camping-grounds were crowded
With caravans of teams;
Then home the jests were driven,
And good old songs were sung,
And choruses were given
The strength of heart and lung.

Oft when the camps were dreaming,
And fires began to pale,
Through rugged ranges gleaming
Swept on the Royal Mail.
Behind six foaming horses,
And lit by flashing lamps,
Old Cobb and Co., in royal state,
Went dashing past the camps.

1 2 8, 423 College of St. Francis Library
Joliet, Illinois

Oh, who would paint a gold-field,
And paint the picture right,
As old Adventure saw it
In early morning's light?
The yellow mounds of mullock
With spots of red and white,
The scattered quartz that glistened
Like diamonds in light;

The azure line of ridges,
The bush of darkest green,
The little homes of calico
That dotted all the scene.
The flat straw hats, with ribands
That old engravings show—
The dress that still reminds us
Of sailors, long ago.

I hear the fall of timber
From distant flats and fells,
The pealing of the anvils
As clear as little bells,
The rattle of the cradle,
The clack of windlass-boles,
The flutter of the crimson flags
Above the golden holes.

Ah, then their hearts were bolder,
And if Dame Fortune frowned
Their swags they'd lightly shoulder
And tramp to other ground.

Oh, they were lion-hearted
Who gave our country birth!
Stout sons, of stoutest fathers born,
From all the lands on earth!

Those golden days are vanished,
And altered is the scene;
The diggings are deserted,
The camping-grounds are green;
The flaunting flag of progress
Is in the West unfurled,
The mighty Bush with iron rails
Is tethered to the world.

CHRISTOPHER BRENNAN

We Woke Together

We woke together on a gusty dawn
in the dim house amid the level waste
and stared in anguish on the stretch of years
filled with grey dawn and ever-weeping wind.

For as the hour hung still 'twixt night and day
we whom the dark had drawn so close together
at that dead tide as strangers saw each other
strangers divided by a waste of years.

We might not weep out our passion of despair
but in lorn trance we gazed upon each other
and wondered what strange ways had brought our hands
together in that chamber of the west.

We felt the dumb compulsion of the hour
to wander forth in spirit on the wind
and drift far apart in undiscovered realms
of some blank world where dawn for ever wept.

Let us Go Down

Let us go down, the long dead night is done,
the dolorous incantation has been wrought,
Soul, let us go, the saving word is won,
down from the tower of our hermetic thought.

See, for the wonder glimmers in the gates
eager to burst the soundless bars and grace
the wistful earth, that still in blindness waits
perfect with suffering for her Lord's embrace.

The spaces of the waters of the dawn
are spiritual with our transfigured gaze;
the intenser heights of morning, far withdrawn,
expect our dream to shine along their ways.

But speak the word! and o'er the adoring whole
straight from the marge of the perfected hours
sudden, large music through the vast, shall roll
a sea of light foaming with seedless flowers;

lilies that form on some ethereal wave
still generate of the most ancient blue,
burst roses rootless, knowing not the grave
nor yet the charnel thought by which they grew.

So we shall move at last, untortured powers,
 and in white silence hear, as souls unborn,
our hymn given back by the eternal Hours
singing together in the eternal morn.

Sweet Silence after Bells

Sweet silence after bells!
deep in the enamour'd ear
sweet incantation dwells.

Filling the rapt still sphere
a liquid crystal swims,
precarious yet clear.

Those metal quiring hymns
shaped ether so succinct:
a while, or it dislimns,

the silence, wanly prinkt
with forms of lingering notes,
inhabits, close, distinct;

and night, the angel, floats
on wings of blessing spread
o'er all the gathered cotes

where meditation, wed
with love, in gold-lit cells,
absorbs the heaven that shed

sweet silence after bells.

My Heart was Wandering

My heart was wandering in the sands
a restless thing, a scorn apart;
Love set his fire in my hands,
I clasped the flame into my heart.

Surely, I said, my heart shall turn
one fierce delight of pointed flame,
and in that holocaust shall burn
its old unrest of scorn and shame.

Surely my heart the heavens at last
shall storm with fiery orisons
and know, enthroned in the vast,
the fervid peace of molten suns.

The flame that feeds upon my heart
fades or flares, by wild winds controlled;
my heart still walks a thing apart,
my heart is restless as of old.

The Years that Go to Make Me Man

The years that go to make me man
this day are told a score and six
that should have set me magian
o'er my half-souls that struggle and mix.

But wisdom still remains a star
just hung within my aching ken,
and common prudence dwells afar
among contented homes of men.

In wide revolt and ruin tost
against whatever is or seems,
my futile heart still wanders lost
in the same vast and impotent dreams.

On either hand life hurries by
its common joy, its common mirth;
I reach vague hands of sympathy
a ghost upon this common earth.

What Do I Know?

What do I know? myself alone,
a gulf of uncreated night,
wherein no star may e'er be shown
save I create it in my might.

What have I done? Oh foolish word,
and foolish deed your question craves!
Think ye the sleeping depths are stirred
though tempest hound the maddened waves?

What do I seek? I seek the word
that shall become the deed of might
whereby the sullen gulfs are stirred
and stars begotten on their night.

How Old is My Heart?

How old is my heart, how old, how old is my heart?
and did I ever go forth with song when the morn was new?
I seem to have trod on many ways, I seem to have left
I know not how many homes; and to leave each
was still to leave a portion of mine own heart,
of my old heart whose life I had spent to make that home.
So I sit and muse in this wayside harbour and wait
till I hear the gathering cry of the ancient winds and again
I must up and out and leave the embers of the hearth
to crumble silently into white ash and dust,
and see the road stretch bare and pale before me: again
my garment and my home shall be the enveloping winds
and my heart be filled wholly with their old pitiless cry.

O Desolate Eves

O desolate eves along the way, how oft,
despite your bitterness, was I warm at heart!
not with the glow of remembered hearths, but warm
with the solitary unquenchable fire that burns
a flameless heat deep in his heart who has come
where the formless winds plunge and exult for aye
among the naked spaces of the world,
far past the circle of the ruddy hearths
and all their memories. Desperate eves,
when the wind-bitten hills turned violet
along their rims, and the earth huddled her heat
within her niggard bosom, and the dead stones

lay battle-strewn before the iron wind
that, blowing from the chill west, made all its way
a loneliness to yield its triumph room;
yet in that wind a clamour of trumpets rang,
old trumpets, resolute, stark, undauntable,
singing to battle against the eternal foe,
the wronger of this world, and all his powers
in some last fight, foredoomed disastrous,
upon the final ridges of the world:
a war-worn note, stern fire in the stricken eve,
and fire thro' all my ancient heart, that sprang
towards that last hope of a glory won in defeat,
whence, knowing not sure if such high grace befall
at the end, yet I draw courage to front the way.

I Said, This Misery Must End

I said, This misery must end:
Shall I, that am a man and know
that sky and wind are yet my friend,
sit huddled under any blow?
so speaking left the dismal room
and stepped into the mother-night
all filled with sacred quickening gloom
where the few stars burned low and bright,
and darkling on my darkling hill
heard thro' the beaches' sullen boom
heroic note of living will
ring trumpet-clear against the fight;
so stood and heard, and raised my eyes
erect, that they might drink of space,
and took the night upon my face,

till time and trouble fell away
and all my soul sprang up to feel
as one among the stars that reel
in rhyme on their rejoicing way,
breaking the elder dark, nor stay
but speed beyond each trammelling gyre
till time and sorrow fall away
and night be withered up, and fire
consume the sickness of desire.

JOHN SHAW NEILSON

Song be Delicate

Let your song be delicate.
  The skies declare
No war—the eyes of lovers
  Wake everywhere.

Let your voice be delicate.
  How faint a thing
Is Love, little Love crying
  Under the Spring.

Let your song be delicate.
  The flowers can hear:
Too well they know the tremble
  Of the hollow year.

Let your voice be delicate.
  The bees are home:
All their day's love is sunken
  Safe in the comb.

34

Let your song be delicate.
  Sing no loud hymn:
Death is abroad . . . oh, the black season!
  The deep—the dim!

To a Blue Flower

I would be dismal with all the fine pearls of the crown of a
    king;
But I can talk plainly to you, you little blue flower of the
    Spring!

Here in the heart of September the world that I walk in is full
Of the hot happy sound of the shearing, the rude heavy scent
    of the wool.

Soon would I tire of all riches or honours or power that they
    fling;
But you are my own, of my own folk, you little blue flower of
    the Spring!

I was around by the cherries to-day; all the cherries are pale:
The world is a woman in velvet: the air is the colour of ale.

I would be dismal with all the fine pearls of the crown of a
    king;
But I can give love-talk to you, you little blue flower of the
    Spring!

Break of Day

The stars are pale.
Old is the Night, his case is grievous,
His strength doth fail.

Through stilly hours
The dews have draped with Love's old lavishness
The drowsy flowers.

And Night shall die,
Already, lo! the Morn's first ecstasies
Across the sky.

An evil time is done.
Again, as someone lost in a quaint parable,
Comes up the Sun.

'Tis the White Plum Tree

It is the white Plum Tree
Seven days fair
As a bride goes combing
Her joy of hair.

As a peacock dowered
With golden eyes
Ten paces over
The Orange lies.

It is the white Plum Tree
    Her passion tells,
As a young maid rustling,
    She so excels.

The birds run outward,
    The birds are low,
Whispering in manna
    The sweethearts go.

It is the white Plum Tree
    Seven days fair
As a bride goes combing
    Her joy of hair.

The Orange Tree

The young girl stood beside me. I
    Saw not what her young eyes could see:
—A light, she said, not of the sky
    Lives somewhere in the Orange Tree.

—Is it, I said, of east or west?
    The heartbeat of a luminous boy
Who with his faltering flute confessed
    Only the edges of his joy?

Was he, I said, borne to the blue
    In a mad escapade of Spring
Ere he could make a fond adieu
    To his love in the blossoming?

37

—Listen! the young girl said. There calls
　No voice, no music beats on me;
But it is almost sound: it falls
　This evening on the Orange Tree.

—Does he, I said, so fear the Spring
　Ere the white sap too far can climb?
See in the full gold evening
　All happenings of the olden time?

Is he so goaded by the green?
　Does the compulsion of the dew
Make him unknowable but keen
　Asking with beauty of the blue?

—Listen! the young girl said. For all
　Your hapless talk you fail to see
There is a light, a step, a call,
　This evening on the Orange Tree.

—Is it, I said, a waste of love
　Imperishably old in pain,
Moving as an affrighted dove
　Under the sunlight or the rain?

Is it a fluttering heart that gave
　Too willingly and was reviled?
Is it the stammering at a grave,
　The last word of a little child?

—Silence! the young girl said. Oh, why,
　Why will you talk to weary me?
Plague me no longer now, for I
　Am listening like the Orange Tree.

Stony Town

If ever I go to Stony Town, I'll go as to a fair,
With bells and men and a dance-girl with the heat-wave in her
  hair:
I'll ask the birds that live on the road; for I dream (though it
  may not be)
That the eldest song was a forest thought and the singer was a
  tree.

Oh, Stony Town is a hard town! It buys and sells and buys:
It will not pity the plights of youth or any love in the eyes:
No curve they follow in Stony Town; but the straight line and
  the square:
—And the girl shall dance them a royal dance, like a blue wren
  at his prayer.

Oh, Stony Town is a hard town! It sells and buys and sells:
—Merry men three I will take with me, and seven and twenty
  bells:
The bells will laugh and the men will laugh, and the girl shall
  shine so fair
With the scent of love and cinnamon dust shaken out of her
  hair.

Her skirts shall be of the gossamer, full thirty inches high;
And her lips shall move as the flowers move to see the winds go
  by:
The men will laugh, and the bells will laugh, to find the world
  so young;
And the girl shall go as a velvet bird, with a quick-step on her
  tongue.

She shall cry aloud that a million moons for a lover is not long,
And her mouth shall be as the green honey in the honey-
    eater's song:
If ever I go to Stony Town, I'll go as to a fair,
And the girl shall shake with the cinnamon and the heat-wave
    in her hair.

Schoolgirls Hastening

Fear it has faded and the night:
    The bells all peal the hour of nine:
The schoolgirls hastening through the light
    Touch the unknowable Divine.

What leavening in my heart would bide!
    Full dreams a thousand deep are there:
All luminants succumb beside
    The unbound melody of hair.

Joy the long timorous takes the flute:
    Valiant with colour songs are born:
Love the impatient absolute
    Lives as a Saviour in the morn.

Get thou behind me, Shadow-Death!
    Oh ye Eternities, delay!
Morning is with me, and the breath
    Of schoolgirls hastening down the way.

I Spoke to the Violet

Shy one, I said, you can take me away in a breath,
But I like not the coat that you come in—the colour of death.

The silence you come with is sweeter to me than a sound,
But I love not the colour—I saw it go into the ground.

And, though you haunt me with all that is health to a rhyme,
My thoughts are as old as the naked beginning of Time.

Your scent does encompass all beauty in one loving breath,
But I like not the coat that you come in—the colour of death.

WILL DYSON

Death is but Death

There is no soft beatitude in Death:
   Death is but Death;
   Nor can I find
   Him pale and kind
Who set that endless silence on her breath.
   Death is but Death!

There is no hidden comeliness in grief:
   Grief is but Grief;
   Nor for thy ill
   Canst thou distil
An unguent from the laurel's bitter leaf.
   Grief is but Grief!

There is no potent anodyne in tears:
   Tears are but Tears;
   Nor can the woe
   Of green wounds grow
Less green for their salt kindness through the years.
   Tears are but Tears!

LEON GELLERT

Before Action

We always had to do our work at night.
I wondered why we had to be so sly.
I wondered why we couldn't have our fight
Under the open sky.

I wondered why I always felt so cold.
I wondered why the orders seemed so slow,
So slow to come, so whisperingly told,
So whisperingly low.

I wondered if my packing-straps were tight,
And wondered why I wondered. Sound went wild . . .
An order came . . . I ran into the night
Wondering why I smiled.

In the Trench

   Every night I sleep
     And every night I dream
   That I'm strolling with my sheep
     By the old stream.

42

Every morn I wake,
    And every morn I stand
And watch the shrapnel break
    On the smashed land.

Some night I'll fall asleep
    And will not wake at dawn.
I'll lie and feed my sheep
    On a green Lawn.

These Men

Men moving in a trench, in the clear noon,
    Whetting their steel within the crumbling earth;
Men, moving in a trench 'neath a new moon
    That smiles with a slit mouth and has no mirth;
Men moving in a trench in the grey morn,
    Lifting bodies on their clotted frames;
Men with narrow mouths thin-carved in scorn
    That twist and fumble strangely at dead names.

These men know life—know death a little more,
    These men see paths and ends, and see
Beyond some swinging open door
    Into eternity.

FURNLEY MAURICE (Frank Wilmot)

To God: From the Warring Nations (Selections)

II

We pray for pity, Lord, not justice, we
  Being but mortal, offer mortal tears,
For justice would mean further cruelty,
  And we have had enough inhuman years.
Guard our repute! We have grown gross and mean,
Who hoped to tell the future something clean!
We come debauched, hoping and hoping not,
  Drunken with blood, burdened with all distress,
Craving for pity, Lord, who have forgot
  The name and manner of sweet gentleness.
We being mortal, love may come again;
Hold back severity—we are but men.
Ah! pity, Lord! Can all indulgence find
  Hope in the devious, devil-ways to Peace,
Of shamefaced, shuddering remnants of mankind
  All murdering, none brave enough to cease?
Redeem us by Thy hope, lest Thy disgust
Makes future empires violate our dust.

III

We've smashed the tablets and the songs, forsworn
  The passionate sweet pity that once reigned
Imperial; must constant fear suborn
  The hearts that guilt and grossness have so stained?
Could we be as we were ere battle came,
We would not talk of guile or separate blame.

44

Search not our records for the first dark ruse,
    Let the past go, sin is an old affair;
We plead for pity, Lord, not for our dues,
    We, being sinners all, must share and share.
Let us, all sinners, and all stained with blood,
    Weary with bitter consciences and lies,
Assemble in a sinners' brotherhood
    And pour out tears from our repentant eyes,
Tears for such wrongs that only tears repair.

V

We have been cruel in thought. Life's not so sweet
    With pearls and pleasures that the race should set
Its ardour to destruction. Brutal feet
    Destroy the roses. God, let us forget
That we accused of barbarous intent
The foe that lies in death magnificent.
How can we hate forever, having proved
All men are bright and brave and somewhere loved?
For every man has courage, all are peerless;
    Each man reigns in his region, sovereign, free;
But we have broken blessed men and fearless,
    Each in his deep and separate agony.
We have cast curses upon unknown names,
    And we have fallen from our vows and Thee,
Gazed tearlessly on tortured human frames,
    And manacled the tongue of equity.
Oh, we have murdered hope and babes and things
Wrought by inspired fingers joyously;
Earth and her vines may shroud our murderings,
    But what shall kill immortal memory?

XV

Thou gavest steel to us, Thou gavest brain,
  Thou gavest patience; we grew grossly great;
And we have used Thy steel Thy will to chain,
  But Thou hast burst those bonds; now we await
Thy judgment, who have meddled with Thy things.
  We thought to snare the sacred flame from Thee—
Look on our broken hands, our withered wings,
  And pity, Lord, our poor humanity.

The Gully (Selections)

II

Looking from the hut door one dawn in June
I saw Australian snow under the moon;
Tall ghostly gums in glacial silence dressed
Towered in eternal rest;
A mass of silver fog, a floating shroud,
Rolled slowly up the hillside to the crest
Like Silence going home into its cloud.
A woodman humped his pack and sauntered west,
Uphill, into the sky,
Where all things go that die
Like flame and sound, and mist and minstrelsy.

VII

There breaks upon my sight
  A low magnificent light
Green as the core that in a green fire burns;
  Each leaf is a green lamp, glowing,
  Swung to illume my going
Down the moist colonnades of mouldering ferns.

Here is a spirit deep,
  Stirring in lonely sleep,
The windswept hills have heard my nameless fear;
  Till by great love oppressed
  I stilled my heart's unrest,
And spoke my love, and speech has brought its tear.

There is a spirit bound
  Within this holy ground;
A chrysalis cares not what freedom brings,
  But, without love or sight,
  Breaks its way into light
Not knowing it will some day move with wings.

X

If I could take your mountains in my heart
And tell the wonder in another land,
As to some mariner mumbling o'er a chart
Strangers would hearken and not understand.
For you, without a poet or a past,
Await establishment; the years seem long
While we by hope and search, by feast and fast,
Prepare the passage for our king of song.
He will not suddenly burst into our day,
He will not come till we have cut the way.
'Tis more than one man's life to strike the reef,
To delve the precious ore, crush out the gold,
Hammer the metal into delicate leaf,
Or link by precious link forge chains that hold
The wandering passions of men in one vast fold.

The Victoria Markets Recollected in Tranquillity

I

Winds are bleak, stars are bright,
Loads lumber along the night:
Looming, ghastly white,
A towering truck of cauliflowers sways
Out of the dark, roped over and packed tight
Like faces of a crowd of football jays.

The roads come in, roads dark and long,
To the knock of hubs and a sleepy song.
Heidelberg, Point Nepean, White Horse,
Flemington, Keilor, Dandenong,
Into the centre from the source.

Rocking in their seats
The worn-out drivers droop
When dawn stirs in the streets
And the moon's a silver hoop;
Come rumbling into the silent mart,
To put their treasure at its heart,
Waggons, lorries, a lame Ford bus,
Like ants along the arms of an octopus
Whose body is all one mouth; that pays them hard
And drives them back with less than a slave's reward.

When Batman first at Heaven's command
Said, 'This is the place for a peanut-stand',
It must have been grand!

48

II

'Cheap today, lady; cheap today!'
Jostling water-melons roll
From fountains of Earth's mothering soul.
Tumbling from box and tray
Rosy, cascading apples play
Each with a glowing aureole
Caught from a split sun-ray.
'Cheap today, lady, cheap today.'
Hook the carcases from the dray!
(*Where the dun bees hunt in droves*
Apples ripen in the groves.)

An old horse broods in a Chinaman's cart
While from the throbbing mart
Go cheese and celery, pears and jam
In barrow, basket, bag, or pram
To the last dram the purse affords—
Food, food for the hordes!

Shuffling in the driven crush
The souls and the bodies cry,
Rich and poor, skimped and flush,
'Spend or perish, buy or die!'

Food, food for the hordes!
The Turksheads tumble on the boards.

There's honey at the dairy produce stall
Where the strung saveloys festooning fall;
Yielding and yellow, the beautiful butter blocks
Confront the poultryman's plucked Plymouth Rocks.

The butcher is gladly selling,
Chopping and slaughtering, madly yelling.
A bull-like bellow for captured sales,
A great crowd surges around his scales.
Slap down the joint.
The finger point
Wobbles and comes alive,
Springs round to twenty and back to five.
To him Creation's total aim
Is selling chops to a doubting dame.
And what will matter his steaks and joints,
The underdone and the overdone,
On the day when old Earth jumps the points
And swings into the sun?

Along the shadows, furtive, lone,
The unwashed terrier carries his week-end bone,
An old horse with a pointed hip
And dangling disillusioned under-lip
Stands in a harvest-home of cabbage-leaves
And grieves.
A lady by a petrol case,
With a far-off wounded look in her face
Says, in a voice of uncertain pitch,
'Muffins', or 'crumpets', I'm not sure which.
A pavement battler whines with half a sob,
'Ain't anybody got a bloody bob?'
Haunted by mortgages and overdrafts
The old horse droops between the shafts.
A smiling Chinaman upends a bag
And spills upon the bench with thunder-thud
(A nearby urchin trilling the newest rag)
Potatoes caked with loamy native mud.

Andean pinnacles of labelled jam.
The melting succulence of two-toothed lamb.
The little bands of hemp that truss
The succulent asparagus
That stands like tiny sheaves of purple wheat
Ready to eat.
Huge and alluring hams and rashered swine
In circular repetitive design.
Gobbling turkeys and ducks in crates,
Pups in baskets and trays of eggs;
A birdman turns and gloomily relates
His woes to a girl with impossible legs.

When Batman first at Heaven's command
Stuck flag-staffs in this sacred strand . . .
We'll leave all that to the local band.

IV

Shuffling in the driven tide
The huddled people press,
Hoarding and gloating, having defied
Hunger, cold and nakedness
For a few days more—or less.
Is it nothing to you that pass?
Will you not pity their need?
Store beef fattens on stolen grass,
Brows grow dark with covetous greed,
Storm or manacle, cringe or pray,
There is no way but the money way.

Pouring suns, pouring heavens, pouring earth,
And the life-giving seas!
Treasure eternally flowing forth,
None greater than these!

Richness, colour and form,
Ripe flavours and juices rare!

Within men's hearts rises a deathless prayer
Deep as a spirit storm,
Giving thanks that the earth has offered such
(So grateful to the eye, so rich to touch)
Miraculous varieties of fare.

And yet that lamb with the gentle eye,
She had to die.
There have been foolish dreams
Of fishes pulled from reedy streams,
Of delicate earthly fruits
Being torn up by the roots—
But only the Mandragora screams.

Gentle curates and slaughtermen
Murder the cattle in the pen:
Body, Spirit, the Word, the Breath
Only survive by so much death.
The old horse with the pointed hip
And disillusioned under-lip
Stands in a drift of cabbage-leaves
And grieves.

WILLIAM BAYLEBRIDGE (William Blocksidge)

Moreton Miles

LIV

Wherever I go, I do no wrong;
My love it burns the same:
So tribes who move the camp along
Carry the guarded flame.

Wherever I go my heart I leave
  With my true Love alone:
I gave it as I vowed to give,
  For others keeping none.

I ask of her like bushmen told
  By travellers of the rain—
Of overlanding mates of old,
  If stirring yet or slain.

Love Redeemed

XXXIII

The utile canons, the set codes of priests,
The scourge the cloister bred, the unbraced employs,
The fatuous passion that for them desists
And gores itself—for growth are such, or boys?
Are these my senses not the appointed gates
To admit joy to my heart? Am I not human?
Health, sensual joy, these Nature consecrates—
Divine, she made me man, my Love a woman.
Nor yet am I all lust, but know a mean:
My fires have settled from their earlier flood;
My veins grow humbler in the sweat I've seen:
Thus can I love her doubting not my blood.
    More sure in this, my full devotion's done—
    With spirit and sense, by love annealed, at one.

LXXXII

Who questions if the punctual sun unbars
Earth's pageant, and flings gold upon the east?
If the swift intersessions of high stars
Make beautiful the night, with magic dressed?

Who asks if grass attires this populous earth?
If leaves put forth their flourish upon trees?
If buds on waking sprays have comeliest birth?
And who, that scans, inquires the why of these?
Who questions, tell, man's breath or blood, that comes
We know not whence, yet is, and dates his day?
These, being, have truth beyond all mortal sums
Of much and less, and prompt nor yea or nay.
    A certitude sublime they have, above
    Belief and non-belief. So has our love.

From *A Wreath*

When tongues will tax me in the public ear,
Or, worse, omit correction for my fault,
When in a wasting grief none standeth near,
Or does so but my poorness to assault,
When flatterers, to pluck me to the bone,
Would break that mail humility has knit,
Or none, my reputation overthrown,
Will tender one up-shouldering word for it,
Or when, the feast done, those assiduous bills
That flocked upon my bread will turn and stab,
O, then I'll mourn the cure for all those ills,
Not found in fortune to be lost in ebb:
I'll mourn thee, friend. But none may put this right;
For Death has sealed thee to perpetual night.

The Ampler Circumscription

Who, not to trifle with his days or blood,
Would set the seal of purpose on his soul
And gather up his parts to amplitude,
Must turn and dedicate him to a goal.
Then, lest he swerve and waste the little light
Or multiply the labour of his load,
So that he come not home before the night,
His feet must know, and straightly tread, the road.
What needeth next? The skill to see what needs,
The power to put impertinence away,
The strength to lift what serveth into deeds—
The auditors of effort, yea and nay.
  The All-wise no offering takes till man hath writ
  The goal, the road, the yea and nay, on it.

Life's Testament

II

The brain, the blood, the busy thews
That quickened in the primal ooze
  Support me yet; till ice shall grip
The heart of Earth, no strength they'll lose.

They take my thought, they laugh, they run—
Ere megatherial moons, begun;
  And shall, till they shall drop within
The shattering whirlwinds of the sun.

In subtle and essential ways,
Rich with innumerable days,
    To mould, to charge, to impel me still,
Each through my broadest being plays.

They surged to this hour, this transfuse—
The brain, the blood, the busy thews;
    That act of mine the ultimate stars
Shall look on sprang in primal ooze.

VI

I worshipped, when my veins were fresh,
A glorious fabric of this flesh,
Where all her skill in living lines
And colour (that its form enshrines)
Nature had lavished; in that guess
She had gathered up all loveliness.
All beauty of flesh, and blood, and bone
I saw there: ay, by impulse known,
All the miracle, the power,
Of being had come there to flower.
Each part was perfect in the whole;
The body one was with the soul;
And heedful not, nor having art,
To see them in a several part,
I fell before the flesh, and knew
All spirit in terms of that flesh too.

But blood must wither like the rose:
'Tis wasting as the minute goes:
And flesh, whose shows were wonders high,
Looks piteous when it puts them by.

The shape I had so oft embraced
Was sealed up, and in earth was placed—
And yet not so; for hovering free
Some wraith of it remained with me,
Some subtle influence that brings
A new breath to all beauteous things,
Some sense that in my marrow stirs
To make things mute its ministers.
I fall before the spirit so,
And flesh in terms of spirit know—
The Holy Ghost, the truth that stands
When turned to dust are lips and hands.

XI

All that I am to Earth belongs:
This Heaven does me violent wrongs.
My fight from fitful loins, my birth,
Are fashioned to the mode of Earth—
Deliberate things, not swiftly given
As some report it falls in Heaven.
This mind is slow to work, this will,
This hand to act them tardier still—
Not dowered with that immediate sense
Deemed in celestial excellence.
True Earth am I, of Earth I'm knit—
O, let me be at peace with it.

XII

Into ethereal meads,
　　Wide azure flowered with stars,
I sped my ravenous soul; it feeds
　　Where end nor check the pasture mars.

And, ranging space, defeat
　　It found not. But, returned,
It knew that vaulting pleasance sweet—
　　Nor health less on this earth it spurned.

Wise thus, it marks, obeys,
　　And honours whence it sprung—
The mighty Being that now stays,
　　That threw it forth, that takes ere long—

The Being that knows not death,
　　The Being that e'er shall be,
Wherein my soul, flesh threading, hath,
　　In force, an Earth's eternity.

Yes, Death is dead; and I,
　　What now, and what before,
On the vast wave of life go by
　　That, reared, shall never reach the shore.

Sextains

The Master-Foe

This let who hate me know, and much admire—
They need not toil to mock me, overthrown:
Long have I led who 'gainst myself conspire;
    And for my wreck suffice I can alone.
    Of all that waste me, no thrust as my own
        Is half so dire.

The Troubled Unquickening

Too beautiful this earth is! Weep I must
    To sense its sureness, and the transience planned
For those I love and me. A doom more just
    (Breath being so swift) had Beauty's violence banned;
    But ah! to know that bliss shall fail not, and
        Our hearts be dust!

MARY GILMORE

Dedicatory

(In Memory of my Father)

I have known many men, and many men
In the quick balance of the mind have weighed.
And even as Abram found his score was ten,
His ten was one, so was my hope betrayed.
But though the tale is told, and fallen spent
Is the first fiction of a great man's name,
Eminent amid the uneminent
He still stands tall; a lonely mark for fame.

So, too, where truth sweeps out time's dusty floor,
I have seen names, long praised, flung out as naught;
And I have seen one, whom the world called poor,
Walking amid the mountains of his thought.

Of Wonder

Give life its full domain and feed the soul
With wonder; find within a clod a world,
Or, gazing on the rounded dewdrop purled
Upon a leaf, mark how its tiny bowl
Includes the sun; that sun in whose control
The planets run their courses, and the furled
Comet, onward driven, resists what hurled
It downward, outward, to its nether goal.

O, as a child, how often have I stood
And watched a turning furrow, beauty spelled!
That rhythm, that curve of moving earth that felled
In endless seam upon the narrowing rood,
Not e'en the sea itself has me so held,
So to my heart brought full beatitude.

Boolee, the Bringer of Life

Breast to breast in the whirling,
Palm to palm in the strife,
Boolee spins over the plain,
Boolee, the bringer of life.

Head to the sky uptowering,
Swift-treading foot on the earth,
Held in his loins the tempest,
Boolee comes, giver of birth.

O Boolee, woman and man!
O Boolee, terror and flame!
Yea against *Nay* in the night,
Out of the whirlwind I came.

The Myall in Prison

Lone, lone and lone I stand,
With none to hear my cry.
As the black feet of the night
Go walking down the sky.

The stars they seem but dust
Under those passing feet,
As they, for an instant's space,
Flicker and flame and fleet.

So, on my heart, my grief
Hangs with the weight of doom,
And the black feet of its night
Go walking through my room.

The Waradgery Tribe

Harried we were, and spent,
Broken and falling,
Ere as the cranes we went,
Crying and calling.

Summer shall see the bird
  Backward returning;
Never shall there be heard
  Those, who went yearning.

Emptied of us the land,
  Ghostly our going,
Fallen, like spears the hand
  Dropped in the throwing.

We are the lost who went
  Like the cranes, crying;
Hunted, lonely, and spent,
  Broken and dying.

The Baying Hounds

There was no hunted one
With whom I did not run,
There was no fainting heart
With which I had not part,
The baying hounds bayed me,
Though it was I was free.

Where'er the hard-prest ran,
Was it or beast or man,
As step by step they went
My breath with them was spent;
The very ant I bruised
My heart held interfused.

Nationality

I have grown past hate and bitterness,
I see the world as one;
Yet, though I can no longer hate,
My son is still my son.

All men at God's round table sit
And all men must be fed;
But this loaf in my hand,
This loaf is my son's bread.

The Dice were Loaded

The dice were loaded full and well
The dreadful night that I was born,
The devils danced a tarantelle,
The whimpering plovers fled the corn.

A fox that hunted hungry food
Lifted his head in ravaged cry;
A shadow ran from out the wood,
In after years that shade was I.

I trod the dark mile all alone,
I trod it lone through all the years;
And but the midnight heard my moan,
And but the bitter earth my tears.

I make no plaint, I make no cry,
No back look give to yesterday;
For, where I saw the hazard lie,
I played the game they bid me play.

And now I hang upon a tree,
My lovely body all forlorn;
The loaded dice were thrown for me
Upon the night that I was born.

The Tenancy

I shall go as my father went,
A thousand plans in his mind,
With something still held unspent
When death lets fall the blind.

I shall go as my mother went,
The ink still wet on the line:
I shall pay no rust as rent
For the house that is mine.

MARY FULLERTON ('E')

A Dream

Unwound the long evolvement,
Mankind was fish again,
Gilled in the fluid prison,
And half absolved from pain.

No rapture and no music,
No agonized despair,
No conscience and no dreaming,
No ecstasies of prayer.

No love to flail the pulses,
Nor love that calms the breast,
But cold mechanic motion,
And cold mechanic rest.

Awake, I cried to heaven,
'God, spin thy spiral fast,
Lest, flinching or lethargic,
Man slides into his past.'

Independence

I resent great instruments
Celebrating my heart's events;
Not for my private joy
Would I a band employ.

I sing my own song
In the high hour;
And when the Dark Power
Bids me be mute,
Yet is a secret lute
Awake in my heart.

Passivity

Call not on comfort lest she come
With all her helpers sleek and dumb—
Soft ropes that seem as frail as air,
To bind you in a cushioned chair,
With anodyne, and balm, and spell,
To chant of droning ritual.

Traffic with danger, heat, and strain,
Face when it comes the spear of pain:
None that achieve—the bad, the good—
Have sold to comfort, hardihood.

O, flaccid, havened, housed, defended,
Flesh still alive, but *living* ended!
Angels nor devils are of these—
The castaways on velvet ease.

Lovers

To be unloved brings sweet relief:
The strong adoring eyes
Play the eternal thief
With the soul's fit disguise.

He will not sleep, and let be drawn
The screen of thy soul's ark;
They keep, those lidless eyes,
Thy sanctuary stark.

God, when he made each separate,
Unfashioned his own act,
Giving the lover eyes
So his love's soul be sacked.

To be unloved gives sweet relief;
The one integrity
Of soul is to be lone,
Inviolate, and free.

Unit

Had Life remained one whole,
Compact of attributes,
Balanced without excess:
Nor men had been, nor brutes.

Had nought been chipped apart,
The fragments found no shapes,
Achieved not temperament:
Men had not been, nor apes.

Undo the forms and lines,
And see the units fall
With prisoned attributes
Back to the primal All.

Oh, gone the tiger's fire,
The blue snake's poison sting,
Each nevermore himself,
But part of everything.

Rob rose of breath and hue,
Diana's limbs unform:
Up, down, and bad and good
Lapped in a pointless norm.

Hope, and desire, and dread,
The mara, and the grapes
Unfeatured, and annulled!
God keep us struggling shapes.

67

Adventure

I heard a halloo in the wood
And went to find who sang;
No elf: but an accoutred wolf
Flashed at me with his fang.

It was a tourney, eye to eye,
Quick staff, and snarling tooth!
Who overcame I cannot tell,
But I emerged forsooth.

My dress and gentle hands were torn;
And, when I reached my door,
There on the lintel was a name
That was not there before.

And now he does not come again,
Who got no welcome in,
But thinking on his signature
I know the might have been.

With life unanswered, heart secure,
I should have lived, and died—
Unknown the mighty Terrible,
Splendid and tawny-eyed.

RODERIC QUINN

The Fisher

All night a noise of leaping fish
Went round the bay,
And up and down the shallow sands
Sang waters at their play.

The mangroves drooped on salty creeks,
And through the dark,
Making a pale patch in the deep,
Gleamed, as it swam, a shark.

In streaks and twists of sudden fire
Among the reeds
The bream went by, and where they passed
The bubbles shone like beads.

All night the full deep drinking-song
Of nature stirred,
And nought beside, save leaping fish
And some forlorn night-bird.

No lost wind wandered down the hills
To tell of wide
Wild waterways; on velvet moved
The silky, sucking tide.

Deep down there sloped in shadowy mass
A giant hill;
And midway, mirrored in the tide,
The stars burned large and still.

The fisher, dreaming on the rocks,
Heard Nature say
Strange secret things that none may hear
Upon the beaten way

And whisperings and wonder stirred,
And hopes and fears,
And sadness touched his heart, and filled
His eyes with star-stained tears:

And so, thrilled through with joy and love
And sweet distress,
He stood entranced, enchained by her
Full-breasted loveliness.

JAMES DEVANEY

Mortality

The lone watch of the moon over mountains old.
Night that is never silent, and none to hark.
Down in the inky pool a fish leaps
With splash of silver light in the liquid dark.

I walk the unknown ways of a foreign land.
The close reeds whisper their secrecies,
And hidden water tunes—earth's oldest voice.
What alien waif is mind among mindless these?

Old, old, everything here is old.
Life the intruder but so briefly stays,
And man the dreamer—soon old changeless time
Will grass his ways.

Fold him, spade him away. Where are they now,
The high courage and love, the laboured store?
Down in the inky pool a fish leapt—
Life is no more.

Winter Westerlies

Leaning against the wind across the paddock ways
Comes Dan home with forward stoop like a man bent and old,
Clashes the door in haste as one pursued: 'By Christ it's cold!'
And crooks his fingers to the blaze.

We do not live these days, but each exhausting day
Unnerved we numbly wait return of life, and must abide
The wind, the still beleaguering wind; all voices else outside
Imperiously it has blown away.

Over the bronze-brown paddocks the grass is bowed flat down;
Along the birdless creek a cold malevolence has passed;
A forlorn sparrow clings on the fence against the icy blast,
His soft breast-feathers loosely blown.

We watch the saplings buffeted without repose,
Their foliage all on one side, plunging without rest,
Stems leaning all one way from the assailing west,
Bending as backs cower from blows.

The hunched cattle no longer feeding dejected stand
With dumb endurance, tails to the flogging wind hour after
        hour;
From some far frozen hell of winds a blind and soulless power
Invades and harries all the land.

The wind! The wind! It fumbles at the fastened panes,
Fills and possesses all, a tyranny without control;
Ceaseless, changeless, malign, searching into the very soul
The rushing desolation reigns.

HUGH McCRAE

Colombine

Exit the ribald clown
   Enter like bubbling wine,
Lighter than thistledown,
   Sweet little Colombine.

     Whisht! and behold the game,
        Long eyes and pointed chin
     Paler than candleflame,
        At her feet Harlequin.

Look how their shadows run,
   Swift as she flies from him!—
Moths in the morning sun,
   Out of a garden dim.

     Faint through the fluttering
       Fall of a flute divine,
     Softly the 'cellos sing
       'Colombine, Colombine.'

Softly the 'cellos sing:
   'Colombine' . . .
   'Colombine' . . .

June Morning

The twisted apple, with rain and magian fire
Caught in its branches from the early dawn,
I, from my bed, through the fogged pane see, and desire
Of its sharp sweetness, something: green the lawn
And stiff with pointed spears of daffodils run wild;
The sluggard sun draws the drowned Daphne back to life—
And all the drowsy doves, brown sparrows, husband, wife,
Are stirring on the housetops—child to early child
Coo-eeing and calling; blind windows open eyes. . . .
And in the air the bitter fragrance floats
Of someone's gardener's pipe; I will arise
And in the stinging shower forget gold motes,
Thick pillows, blankets, books; travel the wholesome road
And give my body to the sun.

Enigma

I watch her fingers where they prance
    Like little naked women, tango-mad,
Along the keys, a cup-shot dance—
    Music, who'll say, more joyous or more sad?

A mystery . . . but not so strange
    As she. Enigma is her pretty name;
And though she smiles, her veiled eyes range
    Through tears of melancholy and shame.

She laughs and weeps. . . . Is it because
    Only tonight she gave herself to me?
The new bud frightened to be glad. . . .
    The child's first vision of the insatiate sea.

73

Song of the Rain

Night,
    And the yellow pleasure of candlelight . . .
    Old brown books and the kind fine face of the clock
    Fogged in the veils of the fire; its cuddling tock.

The cat
    Greening her eyes on the flame-litten mat;
    Wickedly wakeful, she yawns at the rain
    Bending the roses over the pane.
    And a bird in my heart begins to sing
    Over and over the same sweet thing.

    'Safe in the house with my boyhood's love,
    And our children asleep in the attic above.'

Ambuscade

Or the black centaurs, statuesquely still,
Whose moving eyes devour the snuffling mares,
And watch with baneful rage their nervous strides
Whip the dark river white, lest unawares
Some danger seize them. . . . Statuesquely still,
Behind the waving trellises of cane,
The centaurs feel their hearts (besieged with blood)
Stagger like anvils when the sled-blows rain
Shower on shower in persistent flood. . . .

Now Cornus, he, the oldest of the group,
With many wounds, strong arms, and clay-rolled hair,
Coughs for a signal to his dreadful troop,
And springs, wide-fingered, from the crackling lair.

Loudly the victims neigh, they thrash the stream,
They tear their foemen's beards with frothy teeth,
And fill the banks with sparkling spires of steam
That heavenward roll in one tumultuous wreath.

Within the branches of an ancient oak,
A Mother-Satyr, sleeping with her young,
Smit by a sudden stone, upbraids the stroke,
Then turns to see from whence it has been flung.
Scarce does she view the cursed Centaur-pack,
Than, standing clear, she blows a whistle shrill,
Which, like an echo, straight comes flying back
Louder and louder down the empty hill.
A roar of hooves, a lightning-view of eyes
Redder than fire, of long, straight whistling manes,
Stiff crests, and tails drawn out against the skies,
Of angry nostrils webbed with leaping veins,
The stallions come . . .

Morning

The grand red sun has glistened in,
And through the curtain I can see
His disc upon the steeple-pin
(Just touching) of St Anthony.

The night mist on the window flows
In long, wet channels down the pane,
And from the distance slowly grows
The rattle of a country train.

But here, in this disordered room,
The dusty motes stand motionless
Above the glasses in the gloom
That rang last night with merriness.

A spotted spider walks between
The long white fingers of her glove,
Like feathers opened out, to preen,
By some proud thoughtless lady-dove.

Her little sober churchy hat,
Her month-old summer muslin gown,
The short half-stays I marvelled at—
A Frenchman's symphony in brown—

(These, set within a chair, are hid;
A mountain heaped up carelessly—
Sweets hiding other sweets amid
A cataract of lingerie.)

And she herself, still breathing sound,
Her passive eyes fast-closed in sleep,
Waits weary, in her bed, the round
Black Fortune means that she should keep.

Ah frail and sadly beautiful—
Above us in the blue-breast sky
Those stars at dusk most visible
Are now lost treasures to the eye.

And you, a mortal star on earth,
Perhaps, like that bright sisterhood,
So fair by night, may, at the birth
Of Day, be no more where you stood.

And so (that I may see you yet
As when across the lighted Place
Your beauty caught me in its net
And held me by its sovran grace)

I'll leave you softly to yourself
Before a second quarter-chime,
With this memento on the shelf
Until the purple evening time.

Sleep on—your glossy hair unrolled
Burns in my fingers, and I see
A ghostly lover in its gold
Look backward mockingly at me . . .

Another, and another—lo!
Each tress reveals a satyr-face . . .
But I must stop this play and go—
Or choke you with your pillow-lace!

The End of Desire

A flooded fold of sarcenet
Against her slender body sank,
Death-black, and beaded all with jet
Across the pleasures of her flank.

The incense of a holy bowl
Flowed round her knees, till it did seem
That she was standing on the shore
Of some forbidden sunlit stream.

77

A little gong, far through the wall,
Complained like one deep sorrowing,
And from the arras I saw fall
The woven swallow fluttering;

While o'er the room there swam the breath
Of roses on a trellised tree;
Loose ladies in pretended death
Of sweet abandon to the bee.

Flames filled the hollows of my hands;
Red blood rushed, hammering, round my heart,
Like mighty sleds when anvil bands
Gape out, and from their holdings start.

No peace had I, and knew not where
To find a solace that would kill
This pain of flesh so hard to bear,
This sin of soul against the will.

But ever yet mine eyes would seek
That golden woman built for love,
Whose either breast displayed the beak
Through pouted plumes, of Venus' dove.

Her heavy hair, as smoke blown down
Athwart the fields of plenteousness;
Her folded lips, her placid frown,
Her insolence of nakedness.

I took her closely, but while yet
I trembled, vassal to my lust,
Lo!—Nothing but some sarcenet
Deep-buried in a pile of dust.

Fragment

As if stone Cæsar shook
His staff across the wet
Black passages, and took
With marble eyes a yet
Unconquered gaze of Rome;
Marked how the cypress boughs
Stood thick about his home
As when he bent his brows
Three centuries before
Across some Gordian knot
His civic business wore—
Hic jacet the whole lot.

What hammer fell? And whose
The crushed white paper skull
Mixed in the side-bank ooze
Of mighty Tiber . . . Dull
The mind and hand that first
Wrought sparth and sinker-blade,
Knobbed clubs and spikes to burst
The fairy spirit from the shade
He entered in, when through a mesh
Of aching tissues, blood to blood,
And flesh on softly folding flesh,
Man with his woman made a flood
Of kings and weavers, so the world
Might fling about in sunny ways,
Some to the hunt, and some, up-curled,
Stung silent in the martyr's blaze.

79

LEONARD MANN

The Earth

Minute made visible and heard,
  Fact born of space by lust of time,
The aftermath of the first word,
  Mote dried from a drift of slime:

Earth, 'tis enough to know but this,
  You give such beauty to our eyes
And all our senses, here love is
  And the dream-stuff of Paradise.

Your rise in night and your decline
  Sentries nor scientists behold,
No lovers pray of you divine
  Heat for a loved one's heart grown cold.

Yet in illimitable law
  Guessed at by symbols, you may be
Lovely as Venus whom you saw
  This night above your darkening sea.

And where a world has come alive
  May not your littleness be host,
Food of the spirit, the soul's hive,
  Home and haven of Holy Ghost?

Meditation in Winter

Inside the house I sit alone.
The frost will form upon the grass
In meagre paddocks and thin ice
Will glaze the mud and puddles soon.
I see beyond the window-glass
The trees are polished by the moon.

And smoking by the burning log
I grin and wonder how soon I
Will stiffen in death's frost, will lie
Beyond sun's help which, when the fog
Lifts towards next noon, will liquefy
The grass to ripple like a flag.

Believing an escape I made
I left the city yesterday.
Death's grab just missed me on the way.
We passed each other on the road
When the full bus brushed on a dray
That lumbered with a firewood load.

Escape! There is a city in
The fragile fabric of my skull,
This mind, my body's capital,
Whose people sometimes somehow win
To visions strange and beautiful
That fade like dreams before the sun.

Yet like an airman in the night
I see that secret city break
Into a maze of lights and wake
When morning drowns those stars in light,
All gilded and with towers that shake
With bells and tall spires jubilate.

And then know a dead stillness come
And in thick scales the roofs are spread
Upon earth's skin as if some dread
Disease and over it a scum
Of smoke the foul factories feed
Like boils bursting a squalid slum.

There might a river silver run
Through satined shadows and as clear
As in the mountains over there
And shot through long leaves by the sun,
A stream of poetry and lovelier
Than flowed the crystal Helicon.

O if this I could now rebuild
That city to a better plan,
As beautiful as that begun
In dream and then left unfulfilled
When art must put the dream upon
The substance of a real world.

Rebuild that city beautiful,
Rebuild, rebuild it many times,
That city loved in hopes and dreams,
Until its toiling peoples shall
Be changed and so itself redeems
Them for the full life of the soul.

A change strikes on the window-glass:
The wind is risen and the moon
Is lost in heaviest cloud and soon,
I know, the hunched and running grass
Will feel the lashes of the rain
Ere of the sun it comfort has.

E. G. MOLL

Beware the Cuckoo

Beware the cuckoo, though she bring
Authentic tidings of the spring.
And though her voice among the trees
Transport you to the Hebrides!

I saw her come one sunny day,
And pause awhile and fly away,
And I knew where she took her rest
There was a honeyeater's nest.

Later I came again and found
Three dead fledglings on the ground,
And red ants busy in a throng
At throats that had been made for song.

But in the low nest in the tree
The cuckoo chick sat cosily,
And seemed to my unhappy sight
A grey and monstrous appetite.

Beware the cuckoo! By what name
You call her, she is still the same.
And, if you must admire her art,
Keep a wing over your heart.

On Having Grown Old

Now are those peaks unscalable sierras
Against a darkening sky. I may not climb,
Sure of my skill, contemptuous of errors,
Their crags as gaily as once upon a time.
To reach those heights, now, even were I able,
Were but to push a faltering heart too far
And to be laid out at last on a stone table
Bare to the gaze of a mortician star.

No, never again! But from the dull plain counting,
Before dark blot them, every hazardous peak,
I'll let my eyes leap in a swift upmounting
To what I knew, and having known, still seek;
Then, on my slab, while stars put on their white
Uniforms, yield myself to absolute night.

KENNETH SLESSOR

Earth-Visitors

There were strange riders once, came gusting down
Cloaked in dark furs, with faces grave and sweet,
And white as air. None knew them, they were strangers—
Princes gone feasting, barons with gipsy eyes
And names that rang like viols—perchance, who knows,
Kings of old Tartary, forgotten, swept from Asia,
Blown on raven chargers across the world,
For ever smiling sadly in their beards
    And stamping abruptly into courtyards at midnight.

Post-boys would run, lanterns hang frostily, horses fume,
The strangers wake the Inn. Men, staring outside
Past watery glass, thick panes, could watch them eat,
Dyed with gold vapours in the candleflame,
Clapping their gloves, and stuck with crusted stones,
Their garments foreign, their talk a strange tongue,
   But sweet as pineapple—it was Archdukes, they must be.

In daylight, nothing; only their prints remained
Bitten in snow. They'd gone, no one knew where,
Or when, or by what road—no one could guess—
None but some sleepy girls, half tangled in dreams,
Mixing up miracle and desire; laughing, at first,
Then staring with bright eyes at their beds, opening their lips,
Plucking a crushed gold feather in their fingers,
And laughing again, eyes closed. But one remembered,
Between strange kisses and cambric, in the dark,
That unearthly beard had lifted . . . 'Your name, child?'
'Sophia, sir—and what to call your grace?'
   Like a bubble of gilt, he had laughed 'Mercury!'

It is long now since great daemons walked on earth,
Staining with wild radiance a country bed,
And leaving only a confusion of sharp dreams
To vex a farm-girl—that, and perhaps a feather,
Some thread of the Cloth of Gold, a scale of metal,
Caught in her hair. The unpastured Gods have gone,
They are above those fiery-coasted clouds
Floating like fins of stone in the burnt air,
And earth is only a troubled thought to them
That sometimes drifts like wind across the bodies
   Of the sky's women.

There is one yet comes knocking in the night,
The drums of sweet conspiracy on the pane,
When darkness has arched his hands over the bush
And Springwood steams with dew, and the stars look down
On that one lonely chamber . . .
She is there suddenly, lit by no torch or moon,
But by the shining of her naked body.
Her breasts are berries broken in snow; her hair
Blows in a gold rain over and over them.
She flings her kisses like warm guineas of love,
    And when she walks, the stars walk with her above.

She knocks. The door swings open, shuts again.
'Your name, child?'
    A thousand birds cry 'Venus!'

Stars

'These are the floating berries of the night,
    They drop their harvest in dark alleys down,
    Softly far down on groves of Venus, or on a little town
Forgotten at the world's edge—and O, their light
Unlocks all closed things, eyes and mouths, and drifts
    Quietly over kisses in a golden rain,
Drowning their flight, till suddenly the Cyprian lifts
    Her small, white face to the moon, then hides again.

'They are the warm candles of beauty, hung in blessing on
        high,
    Poised like bright comrades on boughs of night above;
They are the link-boys of Queen Venus, running out of the sky,
    Spilling their friendly radiance on all her ways of love.

'Should the girl's eyes be lit with swimming fire,
  O do not kiss it away, it is a star, a star!'
So cried the passionate poet to his great, romantic guitar.

But I was beating off the stars, gazing, not rhyming.
  I saw the bottomless, black cups of space
Between their clusters, and the planets climbing
  Dizzily in sick airs, and desired to hide my face.
But I could not escape those tunnels of nothingness,
  The cracks in the spinning Cross, nor hold my brain
From rushing for ever down that terrible lane,
  Infinity's trapdoor, eternal and merciless.

Five Visions of Captain Cook

I

Cook was a captain of the Admiralty
When sea-captains had the evil eye,
Or should have, what with beating krakens off
And casting nativities of ships;
Cook was a captain of the powder-days
When captains, you might have said, if you had been
Fixed by their glittering stare, half-down the side,
Or gaping at them up companionways,
Were more like warlocks than a humble man—
And men were humble then who gazed at them,
Poor horn-eyed sailors, bullied by devils' fists
Of wind or water, or the want of both,
Childlike and trusting, filled with eager trust—
Cook was a captain of the sailing days
When sea-captains were kings like this,
Not cold executives of company-rules

Cracking their boilers for a dividend
Or bidding their engineers go wink
At bells and telegraphs, so plates would hold
Another pound. Those captains drove their ships
By their own blood, no laws of schoolbook steam,
Till yards were sprung, and masts went overboard—
Daemons in periwigs, doling magic out,
Who read fair alphabets in stars
Where humbler men found but a mess of sparks,
Who steered their crews by mysteries
And strange, half-dreadful sortilege with books,
Used medicines that only gods could know
The sense of, but sailors drank
In simple faith. That was the captain
Cook was when he came to the Coral Sea
And chose a passage into the dark.

How many mariners had made that choice
Paused on the brink of mystery! 'Choose now!'
The winds roared, blowing home, blowing home,
Over the Coral Sea. 'Choose now!' the trades
Cried once to Tasman, throwing him for choice
Their teeth or shoulders, and the Dutchman chose
The wind's way, turning north. 'Choose, Bougainville!'
The wind cried once, and Bougainville had heard
The voice of God calling him prudently
Out of a dead lee shore, and chose the north,
The wind's way. So, too, Cook made choice,
Over the brink, into the devil's mouth,
With four months' food, and sailors wild with dreams
Of English beer, the smoking barns of home.
So Cook made choice, so Cook sailed westabout,
So men write poems in Australia.

II

Flowers turned to stone! Not all the botany
Of Joseph Banks, hung pensive in a porthole,
Could find the Latin for this loveliness,
Could put the Barrier Reef in a glass box
Tagged by the horrid Gorgon squint
Of horticulture. Stone turned to flowers
It seemed—you'd snap a crystal twig,
One petal even of the water-garden,
And have it dying like a cherry-bough.

They'd sailed all day outside a coral hedge,
And half the night. Cook sailed at night,
Let there be reefs a fathom from the keel
And empty charts. The sailors didn't ask,
Nor Joseph Banks. Who cared? It was the spell
Of Cook that lulled them, bade them turn below,
Kick off their sea-boots, puff themselves to sleep,
Though there were more shoals outside
Than teeth in a shark's head. Cook snored loudest himself.

One day, a morning of light airs and calms,
They slid towards a reef that would have knifed
Their boards to mash, and murdered every man.
So close it sucked them, one wave shook their keel,
The next blew past the coral. Three officers,
In gilt and buttons, languidly on deck
Pointed their sextants at the sun. One yawned,
One held a pencil, one put eye to lens;
Three very peaceful English mariners
Taking their sights for longitude.
I've never heard
Of sailors aching for the longitude

Of shipwrecks before or since. It was the spell
Of Cook did this, the phylacteries of Cook.
Men who ride broomsticks with a mesmerist
Mock the typhoon. So, too, it was with Cook.

III

Two chronometers the captain had,
One by Arnold that ran like mad,
One by Kendal in a walnut case,
Poor devoted creature with a hangdog face.

Arnold always hurried with a crazed click-click
Dancing over Greenwich like a lunatic,
Kendal panted faithfully his watch-dog beat,
Climbing out of Yesterday with sticky little feet.

Arnold choked with appetite to wolf up time,
Madly round the numerals his hands would climb,
His cogs rushed over and his wheels ran miles,
Dragging Captain Cook to the Sandwich Isles.

But Kendal dawdled in the tombstoned past,
With a sentimental prejudice to going fast,
And he thought very often of a haberdasher's door
And a yellow-haired boy who would knock no more.

All through the night-time, clock talked to clock,
In the captain's cabin, tock-tock-tock,
One ticked fast and one ticked slow,
And Time went over them a hundred years ago.

IV

Sometimes the god would fold his wings
And, stone of Caesars turned to flesh,
Talk of the most important things
That serious-minded midshipmen could wish,

Of plantains, and the lack of rum,
Or spearing sea-cows—things like this
That hungry schoolboys, five days dumb,
In jolly-boats are wonted to discuss.

What midshipman would pause to mourn
The sun that beat about his ears,
Or curse the tide, if he could horn
His fists by tugging on those lumbering oars?

Let rum-tanned mariners prefer
To hug the weather-side of yards;
'Cats to catch mice' before they purr,
Those were the captain's enigmatic words.

Here, in this jolly-boat they graced,
Were food and freedom, wind and storm,
While, fowling-piece across his waist,
Cook mapped the coast, with one eye cocked for game.

V

After the candles had gone out, and those
Who listened had gone out, and a last wave
Of chimney-haloes caked their smoky rings
Like fish-scales on the ceiling, a Yellow Sea
Of swimming circles, the old man,

Old Captain-in-the-Corner, drank his rum
With friendly gestures to four chairs. They stood
Empty, still warm from haunches, with rubbed nails
And leather glazed, like agèd serving-men
Feeding a king's delight, the sticky, drugged
Sweet agony of habitual anecdotes.
But these, his chairs, could bear an old man's tongue,
Sleep when he slept, be flattering when he woke,
And wink to hear the same eternal name
From lips new-dipped in rum.

'Then Captain Cook,
I heard him, told them they could go
If so they chose, but he would get them back,
Dead or alive, he'd have them,'
The old man screeched, half-thinking to hear 'Cook!
Cook again! Cook! It's other cooks he'll need,
Cooks who can bake a dinner out of pence,
That's what he lives on, talks on, half-a-crown
A day, and sits there full of Cook.
Who'd do your cooking now, I'd like to ask,
If someone didn't grind her bones away?
But that's the truth, six children and half-a-crown
A day, and a man gone daft with Cook.'

That was his wife,
Elizabeth, a noble wife but brisk,
Who lived in a present full of kitchen-fumes
And had no past. He had not seen her
For seven years, being blind, and that of course
Was why he'd had to strike a deal with chairs,
Not knowing when those who chafed them had gone to sleep
Or stolen away. Darkness and empty chairs,

This was the port that Alexander Home
Had come to with his useless cutlass-wounds
And tales of Cook, and half-a-crown a day—
This was the creek he'd run his timbers to,
Where grateful countrymen repaid his wounds
At half-a-crown a day. Too good, too good,
This eloquent offering of birdcages
To gulls, and Greenwich Hospital to Cook,
Britannia's mission to the sea-fowl.

It was not blindness picked his flesh away,
Nor want of sight made penny-blank the eyes
Of Captain Home, but that he lived like this
In one place, and gazed elsewhere. His body moved
In Scotland, but his eyes were dazzle-full
Of skies and water farther round the world—
Air soaked with blue, so thick it dripped like snow
On spice-tree boughs, and water diamond-green,
Beaches wind-glittering with crumbs of gilt,
And birds more scarlet than a duchy's seal
That had come whistling long ago, and far
Away. His body had gone back,
Here it sat drinking rum in Berwickshire,
But not his eyes—they were left floating there
Half-round the earth, blinking at beaches milked
By suck-mouth tides, foaming with ropes of bubbles
And huge half-moons of surf. Thus it had been
When Cook was carried on a sailor's back,
Vengeance in a cocked hat, to claim his price,
A prince in barter for a longboat.
And then the trumpery springs of fate—a stone,
A musket-shot, a round of gunpowder,
And puzzled animals, killing they knew not what

Or why, but killing . . . the surge of goatish flanks
Armoured in feathers, like cruel birds:
Wild, childish faces, killing; a moment seen,
Marines with crimson coats and puffs of smoke
Toppling face down; and a knife of English iron,
Forged aboard ship, that had been changed for pigs,
Given back to Cook between the shoulder-blades.
There he had dropped, and the old floundering sea,
The old, fumbling, witless lover-enemy,
Had taken his breath, last office of salt water.

Cook died. The body of Alexander Home
Flowed round the world and back again, with eyes
Marooned already, and came to English coasts,
The vague ancestral darknesses of home,
Seeing them faintly through a glass of gold,
Dim fog-shapes, ghosted like the ribs of trees
Against his blazing waters and blue air.
But soon they faded, and there was nothing left,
Only the sugar-cane and the wild granaries
Of sand, and palm-trees and the flying blood
Of cardinal-birds; and putting out one hand
Tremulously in the direction of the beach,
He felt a chair in Scotland. And sat down.

Crow Country

Gutted of station, noise alone,
The crow's voice trembles down the sky
As if this nitrous flange of stone
Wept suddenly with such a cry;

As if the rock found lips to sigh,
The riven earth a mouth to moan;
But we that hear them, stumbling by,
Confuse their torments with our own.

Over the huge abraded rind,
Crow-countries graped with dung, we go,
Past gullies that no longer flow
And wells that nobody can find,
Lashed by the screaming of the crow,
Stabbed by the needles of the mind.

Gulliver

I'll kick your walls to bits, I'll die scratching a tunnel,
If you'll give me a wall, if you'll give me simple stone,
If you'll do me the honour of a dungeon—
Anything but this tyranny of sinews.
Lashed with a hundred ropes of nerve and bone
I lie, poor helpless Gulliver,
In a twopenny dock for the want of a penny,
Tied up with stuff too cheap, and strings too many.
One chain is usually sufficient for a cur.

Hair over hair, I pick my cables loose,
But still the ridiculous manacles confine me.
I snap them, swollen with sobbing. What's the use?
One hair I break, ten thousand hairs entwine me.
Love, hunger, drunkenness, neuralgia, debt,
Cold weather, hot weather, sleep and age—
If I could only unloose their spongy fingers,
I'd have a chance yet, slip through the cage.
But who ever heard of a cage of hairs?
You can't scrape tunnels in a net.

If you'd give me a chain, if you'd give me honest iron,
If you'd graciously give me a turnkey,
I could break my teeth on a chain, I could bite through metal,
But what can you do with hairs?
For God's sake, call the hangman.

Sleep

Do you give yourself to me utterly,
    Body and no-body, flesh and no-flesh,
Not as a fugitive, blindly or bitterly,
    But as a child might, with no other wish?
Yes, utterly.

Then I shall bear you down my estuary,
Carry you and ferry you to burial mysteriously,
Take you and receive you,
Consume you, engulf you,
In the huge cave, my belly, lave you
With huger waves continually.

And you shall cling and clamber there
And slumber there, in that dumb chamber,
Beat with my blood's beat, hear my heart move
Blindly in bones that ride above you,
Delve in my flesh, dissolved and bedded,
Through viewless valves embodied so—

Till daylight, the expulsion and awakening,
    The riving and the driving forth,
Life with remorseless forceps beckoning—
    Pangs and betrayal of harsh birth.

Five Bells

Time that is moved by little fidget wheels
Is not my Time, the flood that does not flow.
Between the double and the single bell
Of a ship's hour, between a round of bells
From the dark warship riding there below,
I have lived many lives, and this one life
Of Joe, long dead, who lives between five bells.

Deep and dissolving verticals of light
Ferry the falls of moonshine down. Five bells
Coldly rung out in a machine's voice. Night and water
Pour to one rip of darkness, the Harbour floats
In air, the Cross hangs upside-down in water.

Why do I think of you, dead man, why thieve
These profitless lodgings from the flukes of thought
Anchored in Time? You have gone from earth,
Gone even from the meaning of a name;
Yet something's there, yet something forms its lips
And hits and cries against the ports of space,
Beating their sides to make its fury heard.

Are you shouting at me, dead man, squeezing your face
In agonies of speech on speechless panes?
Cry louder, beat the windows, bawl your name!

But I hear nothing, nothing . . . only bells,
Five bells, the bumpkin calculus of Time.
Your echoes die, your voice is dowsed by Life,
There's not a mouth can fly the pygmy strait—
Nothing except the memory of some bones

Long shoved away, and sucked away, in mud;
And unimportant things you might have done,
Or once I thought you did; but you forgot,
And all have now forgotten—looks and words
And slops of beer; your coat with buttons off,
Your gaunt chin and pricked eye, and raging tales
Of Irish kings and English perfidy,
And dirtier perfidy of publicans
Groaning to God from Darlinghurst.

Five bells.

Then I saw the road, I heard the thunder
Tumble, and felt the talons of the rain
The night we came to Moorebank in slab-dark,
So dark you bore no body, had no face,
But a sheer voice that rattled out of air
(As now you'd cry if I could break the glass),
A voice that spoke beside me in the bush,
Loud for a breath or bitten off by wind,
Of Milton, melons and the Rights of Man,
And blowing flutes, and how Tahitian girls
Are brown and angry-tongued, and Sydney girls
Are white and angry-tongued, or so you'd found.
But all I heard was words that didn't join,
So Milton became melons, melons girls,
And fifty mouths, it seemed, were out that night,
And in each tree an Ear was bending down,
Or something had just run, gone behind grass,
When, blank and bone-white, like a maniac's thought,
The naphtha-flash of lightning slit the sky,
Knifing the dark with deathly photographs.
There's not so many with so poor a purse

Or fierce a need, must fare by night like that,
Five miles in darkness on a country track,
But when you do, that's what you think.

                                    Five bells.

In Melbourne, your appetite had gone,
Your angers too; they had been leeched away
By the soft archery of summer rains
And the sponge-paws of wetness, the slow damp
That stuck the leaves of living, snailed the mind,
And showed your bones, that had been sharp with rage,
The sodden ecstasies of rectitude.
I thought of what you'd written in faint ink,
Your journal with the sawn-off lock, that stayed behind
With other things you left, all without use,
And without meaning now, except a sign
That someone had been living who now was dead:
'At Labassa.   Room 6 × 8
On top of the tower; because of this, very dark
And cold in winter. Everything has been stowed
Into this room—500 books all shapes
And colours, dealt across the floor
And over sills and on the laps of chairs;
Guns, photoes of many differant things
And differant curioes that I obtained . . .'

In Sydney, by the spent aquarium-flare
Of penny gaslight on pink wallpaper,
We argued about blowing up the world,
But you were living backward, so each night
You crept a moment closer to the breast,
And they were living, all of them, those frames
And shapes of flesh that had perplexed your youth,

And most your father, the old man gone blind,
With fingers always round a fiddle's neck,
That graveyard mason whose fair monuments
And tablets cut with dreams of piety
Rest on the bosoms of a thousand men
Staked bone by bone, in quiet astonishment
At cargoes they had never thought to bear,
These funeral-cakes of sweet and sculptured stone.

Where have you gone? The tide is over you,
The turn of midnight water's over you,
As Time is over you, and mystery,
And memory, the flood that does not flow.
You have no suburb, like those easier dead
In private berths of dissolution laid—
The tide goes over, the waves ride over you
And let their shadows down like shining hair,
But they are Water; and the sea-pinks bend
Like lilies in your teeth, but they are Weed;
And you are only part of an Idea.
I felt the wet push its black thumb-balls in,
The night you died, I felt your eardrums crack,
And the short agony, the longer dream,
The Nothing that was neither long nor short;
But I was bound, and could not go that way,
But I was blind, and could not feel your hand.
If I could find an answer, could only find
Your meaning, or could say why you were here
Who now are gone, what purpose gave you breath
Or seized it back, might I not hear your voice?

I looked out of my window in the dark
At waves with diamond quills and combs of light

That arched their mackerel-backs and smacked the sand
In the moon's drench, that straight enormous glaze,
And ships far off asleep, and Harbour-buoys
Tossing their fireballs wearily each to each,
And tried to hear your voice, but all I heard
Was a boat's whistle, and the scraping squeal
Of seabirds' voices far away, and bells,
Five bells. Five bells coldly ringing out.

Five bells.

Beach Burial

Softly and humbly to the Gulf of Arabs
The convoys of dead sailors come;
At night they sway and wander in the waters far under,
But morning rolls them in the foam.

Between the sob and clubbing of the gunfire
Someone, it seems, has time for this,
To pluck them from the shallows and bury them in burrows
And tread the sand upon their nakedness;

And each cross, the driven stake of tide-wood,
Bears the last signature of men,
Written with such perplexity, with such bewildered pity,
The words choke as they begin—

'*Unknown seaman*'—the ghostly pencil
Wavers and fades, the purple drips,
The breath of the wet season has washed their inscriptions
As blue as drowned men's lips,

Dead seamen, gone in search of the same landfall,
Whether as enemies they fought,
Or fought with us, or neither; the sand joins them together,
Enlisted on the other front.

JOHN THOMPSON

Letter to a Friend

Dear George,
        At last the blowfly's buzz retreats,
The sweats of summer fade, the autumn heats
Withdraw their torrid mantle.   Winter comes.
No more the sharp mosquito whines and hums
Around the sleepers in their burning bed.
Keen winter nips them on the nose instead.
The sun, the regular soldier of the sky,
No longer flays us with his angry eye,
For mists and frosts and wild wet winds at last
Return—like friends recovered from the past.

One friend's away.   What reason, what unreason,
Drives you to shun this retrospective season?
You should be here to pledge me drink for drink,
When, by my fire, into my chair I sink:
To bandy joke for joke, while stormy night
Rampages, rages, roars with all his might,
Whips the forsaken streets with whirling rains,
Rattles the doors, and shakes the window-panes.

You should be with me, while the claret flows,
Twisting and stroking your mustachios,
And mingling memories to revive the fun
Of all that we have seen and been and done.

Ah, George, a world of girls has learnt the trick
Since you and I first guttered at the wick;
A world of boys, ruled by unruly glands,
Swaggers and swells in ostentatious stands.
Let them.   For us the ageing interchange
Of slack for tense, of ordinary for strange,
Offers the promise of approaching ease
Where actions fade to reminiscences.
Few have we known who tasted more than us
Folly's extremes or passion's overplus;
Few, too, who braved with such delightful strife
The incalculable cataract of life
To reach the central torrent, the clear sweep
Of confident waters channelling smooth and deep
Beyond all idle pools and foolish froth.

One truth we firmly hold, upon my oath,
(Not only for ourselves, for others too)
That each should do as he desires to do.
Inland and northward (would that you were here)
Nature walks with a blossom at each ear;
So, though my fire be snug, my cellar rich,
I cannot blame you for your restless itch.
Old though you be in every chromosome,
Go on, go further; for the more you roam
The finer fables you will bring back home.

Where are you drinking now, with rosy face?
In what unmapped or half-forgotten place
Plotting a detour of a thousand miles
To hunt for folk-songs or for crocodiles?
Upon what mangrove beach or coral cay
Animal-naked all the livelong day?
Above what mountain, borne on silver wings,
Flying your thirst to Broome or Alice Springs?

Mean minds, though they may cage the hawk or fox,
Cannot keep radium in a cardboard box;
They cannot strap up gales or gag the thunder
Or screw down clamps to hold an earthquake under;
Much less can they emasculate or kill
Man's giant affection, his titanic will,
Or the huge Joy that drives him up the cliffs
Of the most wild Perhaps and dangerous Ifs.
Dullness and Hatred, meeting no resistance,
Lose themselves in emptiness and distance,
But vital Gusto, bursting from duress,
Prospers in unrestraint and boundlessness.

Rejoice, dear George, in freedom.   I admit
That, were you here, we'd talk with better wit
Of what we wish for than of what we did,
Long since, in bright Papeete or Madrid.
Above my roof the wrathy weather rolls;
Within, red orchids bloom among the coals.
Down the wet street belated taxis hiss;
Within, is warmth.   Only yourself I miss.
Were I with you, how rousing it would be,
Over some murmuring moonlit tropic sea,

To steer for scenes unvisited before,
Cuzco, Mauritius, Bangkok, Travancore.
Enough, enough! Don't tempt me any more!
Lóth as yourself the tether's length to learn,
I drink (from this full glass) to your return.

ROBERT D. FITZGERALD

From *Copernicus*

The cock that crowed this dawn up, heard
along the east an earlier call
as through sunk acres bird by bird
till imminent upon sleep's coast
day-urgent messages were tossed,
forerunners of the flaring ball;

and reckoned thus: 'Let one voice fail
our sacred task, then drowns the sun;
nor could the parted chain avail
to fish him forth or in the least
appease that Rooster of the East
by whom first daylight is begun.

So, stern like destinies, we bear
the signals westward without bound;
and always heralds waiting there
will stretch and flap and pass the shout,
and still no last . . . whence—reason it out—
last is new first; the world's egg-round!

Boast across morning each to each
this toil has made our proud estate
far other than old fables teach
which call us puppets jerked for sport;
cry, every bird is in some sort
that leader clamouring at dawngate.'

Essay on Memory

Rain in my ears: impatiently there raps
at a sealed door the fury of chill drops—
knuckles bared of the flesh come rattling on
vaults that conceal a sorrier skeleton
huddled, unhearing, in a dark so deep
that this clear summons ruffles not calm sleep.

It is the hand of Memory come scratching
on the tomb of carrion buried from mankind—
forgotten by all except this body-snatching
walker of old night and times dropped from mind,
who knows where the slain rots and seeks it yet;
for Memory does not fail though men forget,
but pokes a ghost-finger into all our pies
and jabs out the dead meat, a grim Jack Horner,
mocking the mild dream, half guess, half lies,
of History babbling from his chimney-corner.

Memory is not that picture tacked on thought
among the show-girls and prize-ribbon rams,
wherein is last week's yesterday to be sought,
lens-twisted and fading, and yet somehow caught
in the known gesture, almost at speaking terms;
nor is it the sky-old story which in stone

within baked saurian footmarks prints its own,
as if the mud might soften and recollect
almost our lean beginnings and project
against the background of these days some far
horrible firmament, or show a star
choking with cloud whereunder, oozed from slime,
slow forms are dragging—half-way back through time;
nor is it composite mind whose cells are men
and whose dour genius grafts great stone on stone
by torch-flare lit on torch-flare—till it seems
that the tall topwork of new cornice gleams
in the glow of ancient lore, and sits firm-stayed
in masonry that hands long cold once laid.

Something of all this . . . but Memory peers
from the brown mottled ruin, shrieks and gibbers
among the fallen fragments of lost years,
lurks by the lichened archway, frights the neighbours
when a wind shrills about that older house
on which these days have quarried and made levies.
For Memory is the wind's voice in the crevice,
a wild song through those stones and in the boughs
of trees fast-dug in flint-chips of the novice;
it is the count of hooves for ever dinned
in the ears of the world by the hard-ridden wind;
and more than these and more than headlong haste
of events galloping through widening waste
into the cumulative past—to keep
galloping on with never pause nor sleep—
it is the past itself, the dead time's will
poisoning today's pulse and potent still;
it is the ruled heart's heritage, mortmain;
darkness it is and talons of the rain.

And under earth, so varied and so golden
telling must halt, lie jars which life's old trouble
brimmed gaily, which have felt that wine embolden
hopes that looked out on many a morning olden.
And were they dupes of the dawn, then, seeing double,
since all are smashed, the false clay like the noble,
knaves and brave men all gone, and dainty wenches?
Not, surely, while the grape yet spurts one bubble,
though vessels crack and are pushed down from their benches.
And these that there lie shattered, and their nights,
rapturous, and their days, or meek as prayer,
or polished like hard brass by glinting lights,
fell, each, before some fumbling hour, their slayer.
Now is the spread stain of their deaths long vanished
and the wine froths again and never gayer,
though theirs is all soaked up, dank earth replenished,
so it might seem the book closed, the tale finished;
yet are they loot of Memory, who comes
unrecognised from rifling those bleak tombs . . .
Stranger at the door, like doom, disaster,
no man can bar you out, this house's master.

*   *   *

In our own garments left to face the drear
whinings of winter, stripped of gauds and gear
save what is patently our due and worn
by rights inherent, cold indeed were morn,
naked were noon. No comfort could we claim
except from that one wavering inward flame
unquenched through change and time, which though it
     wrought
in intricate iron the twisted chain of thought,
link by link stretching, vagrantly designed,

back past first hammerings of conscious mind,
is yet so fine, for all its intense white core,
stretched fingers freeze which were but chilled before.

(Strange miracle of self, mysterious, lit
no man knows how nor whence uprises it!
Lamp by lamp flickers out; this flame burns on
here—yet remotely here—and ever alone,
freezing and powerless, too, for each isled spark
were little avail against the encroaching dark
and life would perish on its pavement-flags
but that we clasp about us cast-off rags
and robes of dead kings . . .)
                              Rain over the world:
one handspan counts a million splashes hurled
minute by tireless minute; yet these are
random and wayward only, scattering far.
Denser, outnumbering the raindrop prisms,
there's a dumb deluge driven across night's chasms,
hard in upon us, unresisted, beating
our lives to patterns imposed past all defeating
by our poor wills; we are storm-carried, storm-shed,
battered by streaming multitudes of these dead.

They are about us on all sides: the dust
is restless; the bruised tongues of trodden weeds
speak with harsh voices, menace; grass-blades thrust
at parrying air that mirrors bygone deeds;
and who might think the unquiet is, at most,
wistful backgazing of the unbodied host,
homesick for life, who tread some screened-off path
of supernatural being beyond death,
let him once clutch at his own arms, so trussed

in thongs of old inheritance they can
but move in those accustomed tasks of man
allotted, limited, by the flesh they wear
ancestrally; he'll find an answer there,
fragile for sure, yet tougher than a ghost.

Indeed, we are the substance of their thought
which starves in air, can balance on no mystic
knife-edge of abstract being, twixt nought and nought,
so kneads itself in this inert, this plastic
material of our lives. But reckoning so,
farther and farther back, bared long-ago
which spores in shafts of time and mushroom-swells
through midnight-centuries, sees all things else
not as existence, but as forms worked over
in one huge bulk ere each is lost for ever,
not as reality but its escape
in impress after impress of pure shape,
and so dissolves the world. Now only appear
re-shuffling motion and the turn of the year;
all is become sheer action which perceives
bright leaves themselves as rustling of the leaves,
the bird's flight as the bird. This, heart denies
eternally; and Memory, too, replies—
links up the many flights upon one thread
of keen-eyed bird too busy to be dead
between flights done; for Memory stays the hour
and behind flower-growth is even the flower.
And we ourselves are Memory, and retain
so much of those gone, the little death can gain
is found a cheat of the senses; change and birth
convulsive writhings of autophagous earth.

* * *

Argument is the blade-bright window-pane
which shears off cleanly the slant sheaf of rain,
and in the room heart's dream and life's desire
are radiance and curled, unfolding fire.
Here thought may ponder in peace or work at will
or take down book from shelf and read his fill;
but though among men's assets he bides long
always his ears are tuned on that same song
of rain outside; for that's the force he knew
which drenched his hands that battled it, breaking through,
while yet he was homeless in the world, unsafe,
wandering in mindless marshes the wind's waif,
and had not learned to build up words and fix
a house for himself in speech's bonded bricks.
Hearing it, he remembers: though large walls
shelter him now, hold out the rain, rain falls.

And ever the untaught earth, comrade of yore,
out there under the dark and dripping leaves,
although its slave-bent back, laid bare, receives
whip-stripes of rain, possesses yet that more,
wisdom and fullness, which thought has not known,
never can reach. For earth, stooped labourer,
treading the furrow of seasons, early astir
and late abed from heavy fields, wild sown,
has wind and sun for sure realities,
endures this lash, too, as a thing plain-shown,
simple as flooded rivers, tumbling seas,
gaunt hills across the sky . . . These are earth's own;
but thought has only sounds and shadows thrown
by hollow powers, obscure immensities,
upon the screen called living. And the good, solid
meat that earth munches, truth, is proved invalid;

thought is unfed—and even thought has grown
a trifle impatient of philosophies . . .

And mourns, like Memory, old simplicities,
other truth yet, as stark as in years younger
trod the wet clay—till this plain truth of hunger
cries: 'Time to rouse! Put by the reading-glass
which showed up print so clearly, a jagged mass
of black rocks in a dangerous foam of white,
showed more than sight could know, but not like sight,
split into jutting patches the blunt sense
and took more note of blots than eloquence.
Time now to trust our eyes, which if they find
less than the glass, less than contents the mind,
have yet their own sure knowledge of shape and fact
not as things purely are, but as they act.
And well to go among men, see how they do
the will of the past and bend their backs thereto,
the past that guides them, rules them, flogs—and flings
a despot's largesse, treasure of spoiled kings.
See how they walk between a day and a day,
command the future, and the past obey,
their present only a footing on some height
that fronts new dawn for ever, dazed with light;
see how their knowledge, between night and night,
asks, but not answers, whither winds the way.'

*   *   *

If, as may seem, fair future spreads unfurrowed
beneath new morning and there writhes and wheels,
a sun-blind sea all silverly tomorrowed,
ruffled by promise and uncut by keels,
and, Dampiers of this dawn, we pull the prow
off-wind and pay out sheet, none tells us now

what bides our choice or if we drown or starve;
and even if the luck holds and we carve
new coasts on gaping latitudes, who traces
the scarless wake of an adventurer, lost,
sows wheat, finds gold, where we found desert places,
gashes with screws wide lanes where, lone, we crossed?

This hour, a gulp in the long throat of the past,
swallows what once was future, but soon spent;
this hour is a touch of hands, an accident
of instants meeting in unechoing vast:
it is a rail that bursts before the flourish
of black manes and time's haste; it fails our need—
now must decision be brief, must jump or perish
under the feet and fury of stampede.
And to this difficult present will succeed
what present, to be lost as this is lost?
for any decision may fall undermost,
and no hand counts the grandsons of its deed.
Foresight is but a bargain that we make,
which, even should life keep it, death will break.

*   *   *

Who sees this time all edged about with wars
like tiny points of fire along the rim,
stretching to suns then sinking back to stars,
must hold heart-close his love to speak for him
and be his challenge to those rigorous teeth
that devour all, the answer of his faith—
which is towards the green-burst of new spring,
leaf-revelry and flower-strewn roistering,
life-joy and the dear miracle of increase.
Yet who stares forward through the shimmer of peace,

noon-heavy over valleys soaked in health,
and, baulked of sight beyond this burgeoning wealth,
finds only tremor-tapestry, hung haze,
will watch, adread, for the first beaconing blaze.
Or if the only smokes that, serpentine,
encoil the land be stubble-fires that twine
ribbons of incense round a harvest-feast,
still must one fear be troublous, one at least—
a vision of changed scene wherein smokes, black,
crawl venomous from a Gorgon chimney-stack,
with, deep below, all foreign to our ken,
strange engines and strange customs and strange men!

Well might our senses shudder when flesh hears
the coming Unseen, the spectre-march of years;
for though a man face fortunes horror-haunted,
gruesome with prophecies, and grin undaunted,
shall he bear blame from the accusing eyes
of legions grey with agony? bear their cries
sinking in floods of fire he dreams not of
and has condemned them to in very love?
Well may he see his children, such a one,
and groan doubt-drunkenly: 'What have I done?'

Rain in the clean sun falling—riches of rain
wash out the dusty fear, the air's dull stain;
ay, Memory is a shower of gilded darts
which pins today's delight on our healed hearts,
or, in our hands, is mintage of bright faith:
shame on us to be beggared by a wraith!
Now, till this trove be gone, the last coin sped,
doubt were a glum ingratitude to the dead.

How should we hold us from wild enterprise,
who use the limbs of the past and its quick eyes
and are eternally in debt to those
who stung into the earth-dawn's turgid throes
urge of keen life? We'll crash the trestles down
that barricade clear laughter, take the town
on a burst of shouting that through fissures rent
cascades its fervid glee, magnificent.
We'll slit gloom's gullet, oracling defeat,
and crack great barrels of song in open street,
free for the drinking. We'll make fabulous
this world, in honour of them who gave it us,
not just the Nelsons, Newtons, of our race,
the Phillips grounding at a landing-place
continent-wide, but all whom violence of mind,
violence of action, gave such singleness
that if they did but grow, ambitionless
except to live in the sun, they served their kind
with that straight growth of will which bears for seed
zest to create; which, grasping at blind air,
graves flowers from veriest nothing and makes fair
all that we have. Theirs was that splendid greed,
hewer of men and vineyards, nation-maker,
destroyer of hate and weakness, tyrant-breaker,
whose slow attrition, whetstone of advance,
grinds laws, arts, customs, from steel circumstance.

Then knot this hour's activity as a rope
in strength of climbing hands; for still our hope
best clings to shoulders swarming—from the mouth,
black-gaping, of loss and failure; all we know
is this jerked ladder of change whereby men go
with gasping struggle, vigour of movement—up!

Wherefore all good is effort, and all truth
encounter and overcoming . . .
              We whose scope
clasps the tremendous leagues of summer-south,
thunder-oppressive with curbed energies,
least of all folk need question our day's worth
or think its turmoil twitchings of spent earth.
Here noon above burnt, bony ridges hung
nerve-tense, is strident with an unheard tongue,
pregnant with daring and with destinies;
and the mist-floating islands and raw seas
nigh us and those strained ranks of shores far-swelling
knit us with fortunes idle the foretelling.
And though we plan and make, for we would keep
won soil a little beyond the ruptured sleep
of bursting tomorrows gonged upon our ears,
it is little to hold this land star-counted years
or even tonight yield it; much that fever
pounds along resolute limbs its scorching river—
doings, upheavals—much that skies, bow-drawn,
are tautened by red-eyed but still tireless dawn . . .

          Whatever the task, it lies in front: we must
build upward though we guess not to what skies,
and though the eruptive Babels that we thrust
vital in air will fritter back to dust;
else we betray the lamp behind our eyes,
the quickening in our veins, both held in trust
since long before the scumming of the germ
upon first seas. We will serve out our term:
not yet the impetus flags whose course began
when at the blank mouth of our stinking lair
we saw night's infinite curtain shake with grey,

and so went forth determined to be Man,
standing at last erect, and watched new day
wrap back the dark and strip the valley bare.

So, should our best work fail us, walls we planned
stifle in years blown over fine like sand,
or life itself reach gulfs and lorn extremes—
even some crag of ending—where bled dreams
kite in the wind weightless and the past
unclaws our very world, lets go at last,
but still remains, being Memory, one live link
of gone with all-to-come, and from the brink
peers out beyond; then, launched above that steep,
venture shall cant bold wings and with their sweep
splinter such clogging silence as they met
in older abyss where time slept stirless yet.

1918–1941

Not those patient men who knocked and were unheeded
where ignorance impeded like a flat panel swung
before the tower-stair to the dark mind of the young:
another moved beside them on the dais, at the desk—
War in a square cap, gowned and grotesque.

This was the master whose tongue did the talking:
then time became a chalking-off of dates upon the wall—
for no lad chose a calling who heard instead a call,
and just beyond a boy's years (so the lesson ran)
the one work waited fitting for a man.

None grew so tiptoe as to see the plain road, yonder,
at the hour's edge dip under to the leagues of calm before.
It was odd to break step and shamble from the door,
to plough the broad peace, and grow older, and learn pride
from the day's task met and the morrow still defied.

Distant the guns are and no wind veering
has brought them into hearing, nor yet in these lands
do they bawl between hills as between a pair of hands;
but here's what we were bred to . . . and strange it is then
to be lifting our sons up to watch the marching men.

Tattered the bewilderment I pull across my shoulders
and, shamed before beholders in this torn shirt,
like a slave to my shoes I wander unalert,
with eyes but no thought in them to mark the way I tread,
and a thought without eyes that runs lost in my head.

The Face of the Waters

Once again the scurry of feet—those myriads
crossing the black granite; and again
laughter cruelly in pursuit; and then
the twang like a harpstring or the spring of a trap,
and the swerve on the polished surface: the soft little pads
sidling and skidding and avoiding; but soon caught up
in the hand of laughter and put back—

There is no release from the rack
of darkness for the unformed shape,
the unexisting thought
stretched half-and-half

in the shadow of beginning and that denser black
under the imminence of huge pylons—
the deeper nought;
but neither is there anything to escape,
or to laugh,
or to twang that string which is not a string but silence
plucked at the heart of silence.

Nor can there be a floor to the bottomless;
except in so far as conjecture must arrive
lungs cracking, at the depth of its dive;
where downward further is further distress
with no change in it; as if a mile and an inch
are equally squeezed into a pinch,
and retreating limits of cold mind
frozen, smoothed, defined.

Out of the tension of silence (the twanged string);
from the agony of not being (that terrible laughter
tortured by darkness); out of it all
once again the tentative migration; once again
a universe on the edge of being born:
feet running fearfully out of nothing
at the core of nothing:
colour, light, life, fearfully
becoming eyes and understanding: sound becoming ears . . .

For eternity is not space reaching
on without end to it; not time without end to it,
nor infinity working round in a circle;
but a placeless dot enclosing nothing,
the pre-time pinpoint of impossible beginning,
enclosed by nothing, not even by emptiness—

impossible: so wholly at odds with possibilities
that, always emergent and wrestling and inter-linking,
they shatter it and return to it, are all of it and part of it.
It is your hand stretched out to touch your neighbour's,
and feet running through the dark, directionless like darkness.

Worlds that were spun adrift re-enter
that intolerable centre;
indeed the widest-looping comet
never departed from it;
it alone exists.
And though, opposing it, there persists
the enormous structure of forces, laws,
as background for other coming and going,
that's but a pattern, a phase, no pause,
of ever-being-erected, ever-growing
ideas unphysically alternative
to nothing, which is the quick. You may say hills live,
or life's the imperfect aspect of a flowing
that sorts itself as hills; much as thoughts wind
selectively through mind.

The eggshell collapses
in the fist of the eternal instant;
all is what it was before.
Yet is that eternal instant
the pinpoint bursting into reality,
the possibilities and perhapses,
the feet scurrying on the floor.
It is the suspense also
with which the outward thrust
holds the inward surrender—
the stresses in the shell before it buckles under:

the struggle to magpie-morning and all life's clamour and lust;
the part breaking through the whole;
light and the clear day and so simple a goal.

Traditional Tune

Though moonlight dapples
past time-effacement
the harbour ripples,
the candied air,
it's all deserted—
like lover from love's casement
there has departed
what found these fair.

Yet where I follow
some few hours older
and call youth shallow
from wisdom's crutch,
Life meets me, gaudy,
a rose pinned at her shoulder
for hands as greedy
as once dared touch.

O moondrowned city
be long of learning
that graver ditty
than old delight—
that song of mortals
of—over springs returning—
the flash that hurtles
through upper night.

J. A. R. McKELLAR

Twelve O'Clock Boat

Only the creaking murmur of the wheel,
The trembling of the engines as they turn;
The ferry glides upon an even keel,
And Pinchgut squats in shadow hard astern . . .

The lips of ocean murmur at delay.
The lovely moon no longer will refuse,
And from the arms of darkness slips away
To tryst with young Ephesians on Vaucluse,

Naked as when some mercenary Greek
The galleys bore to Carthage stared the sky,
Feeling a wind Sicilian on his cheek,
And fell asleep with no more hope than I

Of life eternal, love, or length of days,
Dreaming he saw his Macedonian home;
Awoke, and duly went his ordered ways
To die at Zama, on the swords of Rome.

But what was moon to him, and what was sea
Two thousand years before myself was born,
Are sickle moon and silver yet to me,
Though Scipio should wait upon Cremorne.

ETHEL ANDERSON

Migrants

I was even wearier where I waited
In the noontide heat for the coming of night
Than the wedge-tailed swallow, the sea wayfarer,
Tired of wind and planet and the fading wave;

I knew no such solace as I've known them flailing
From the nick of moments in an edgeless sky,
Birds linked in the eddies of the Empyrean
To ease the spent fledgling and the failing wing;

Yet the bright Siberian snow they nest by,
The plaited rainbow of the Samarkandh lane,
Mean less to the wanderers pressing towards them
Than to me the homelight as I look backward.

PETER HOPEGOOD

Free Martin

Here is Martin's round house;
built it is of mud.
From the lake he won it
with his hod and spud.

Came the elphin hunters
following the deer
over fell and moorland
over half a year.

Panting from the lakeside
hard before the din
comes a bonny roebuck.
Martin takes it in.

When the chase has dwindled,
Martin: says the roe;
Ask for what you will . . .
it is yours before I go.

I would like a gorget
ruddy as your coat.
I would like a white horse,
I would like a boat.

I would like a mantle
deep and dark and blue;
I would like a sharp arrow
to sever it in two.

I would like a portcullis
to set before my gate.
I would like a bonny doe
to be my bonny mate.

You shall have a gorget
ruddy as the sun;
And a horse as white as foam
and a boat, in one.

You shall have a portcullis
to set before your keep.
You shall have a silver doe
to rouse you from your sleep.

You shall have a mantle
deep and dark and blue;
you shall have a sharp arrow
to sever it in two.

Yet I charge you answer
this before I go:
Who shall wear a cloak shent
by a sharp arrow?

Martin gives for answer:
Just before the dawn
comes a naked fellow
and lays him on the lawn.

Bloody are his limbs and crown;
bloody is his track;
and cold . . . cold . . . cold
blows the wind from off the lake.

I would share my mantle
dark and blue and deep
with that bloody cold one
who troubles all my sleep;

for he may not enter here.
His place is on the lawn.
And cold . . . cold . . . cold
blows the wind about the dawn.

He should have my mantle
dark and deep and whole.
He should have its blue unshent
would it warm his soul.

But 'twould noways warm him,
not in any part,
without its sister portion
be warmed by my own heart.

His pallid breast it will not warm
into a living glow
without my own be smote in twain
by a sharp arrow.

Blood must drench our mantle
deep and dark and blue . . .
blood must stain our mantle
to a kingly hue.

His bloody limbs it may not heal
of the red wounds they bear
from the bolts of Elphin
over half a year,

until the Livid Hunter
hanging on the Oak
shall launch a levin swift to sear
in twain a seamless cloak.

Gi'n I gain our mantle
deep and dark and blue,
gi'n I gain a sharp arrow
to sever it in two,

I shall have my white horse,
I shall have my boat,
I shall have a sunrise
darting from my throat,

I shall have a portcullis
to set before my keep
and a bonny doe with coat aglow
to rouse me from my sleep.

Dithyramb in Retrospect

I was carried to a font.
Stranger fingers marked my front.
  Significant, no doubt, the rite
  that day was day and night was night:
  yet it could not make me see.
  Lifeless was that sorcery.

Then I sought a font in Toil,
smeared my sweaty brows with Soil.
  Still by fingers strange 'twas done,
  though the fingers were my own.

Then I sought a font in Fire;
leapt I Armageddon's pyre.
  Iron set on me his hand:
  but 'twas still a stranger brand.

Then a passion smote my heart
with a devastating dart.
  Still I could in no wise see.
  Darkness ever compassed me.

With my pain I face the Sky
When my planet there must ply . . .
  And the fingers of the wind
  touch me with my Very Wand.
  Straightway know I power to see
  what the light has hid from me.

By the Wind that walks the Night
I am baptized into sight.

MAX DUNN

Flower of Exile

Now wanderer in hostile forests, exile
By choice among unchosen enemies,
Beneath the crooked moon he still goes seeking
On boughs of flesh the flower that never dies.
On his grey screen unfolds no daylight image,
No undistorted archetype of peace,
Except blurred letters on a broken column,
Buried where now green silences arise,
And the far-off tolling of a bell sunken
Among ships' bones and red anemones.
Yet, in a long-forgotten garden, the seed
He tossed upon a heap of stones still lies,
Its golden burden undelivered, waiting
Till he returns from barren voyages:
The lock is green with time, the key is rusted,
But through the gate sleeps his lost paradise.

I Danced Before I Had Two Feet

I danced before I had two feet
And sang before I had a tongue;
I laughed before I had two eyes
And loved before my heart was young.

I swam before I had two hands
And held the distance in my toes
Before I heard the stars or knew
The wild compulsion of the rose.

I bore the fruit of many lives
Before I came into this day;
I knew before my grave was made
The worms eat only death away.

FRANCIS BRABAZON

Victoria Market

I said to my companion, this is walking
I said to my companion, how my heart goes
    out to all lovers.

The darkness was still warm
but the fields were freshening beautifully
    in the winter rain;
the market was full of little lights
and I remarked the ear of a sack
sleeping on top of a tyre like a cat
    on the kerbstone

I said to my friend stop falling on your knees
I have to keep pulling you on to your feet again—
   then the dawn came down silently between
   the rows of vegetables
and we passed out into the white star
rejoicing companionless in our love

As I crossed the square on my way home
the highest spires were ablaze with the movement of feet.

BRIAN VREPONT

The Net-menders

I came upon them by a strip of sea,
In a drizzle of rain mending their fishing-net,
Four swift brown hands, and lean with industry,
Shuttling the thin twine skilfully in-out, repairing the fret
Of rock-jag, shark-tooth and thresh;
He, tense as a mackerel, strong and agile,
Sea-eyed and grim as a rock, turned, and his smile
Was as the wonder of sunshine on sea-rock,
His fingers harping the net-mesh;
She on the sea-side, facing the land, took stock
Of me leisurely nearing, through half-shut eyes.
'Defence', I thought; but her mouth relaxed, went sweet
And soft as a sea-flower, her hands' enterprise
On the sea-side of the breaks in the net
Rippling the strings of the two-sided harp o' the sea,
And I thought, 'Here is where sea-melodies meet,
Mending the breakages of earth-and-sea-fret,'
And the strange great grace of simplicity came on me.

If they had angers in them, these two by the sea,
Not in the two days dwelt with them,
Watching the shuttle flying, the flat corks tied,
And the strong boat pitch-caulked for battle with the sea,
Was flaw apparent in the gem;
Their poverty, too real for pride to hide,
Gave them no envy, not even in the lamp-light
And shadows of our talk,
Not when the net was trailed and netted nought
Save weed, nor when I spoke, that unforgettable night
We fought the tide, and drifted home star-caught,
And I spoke of the hawk
Now in the dark vanished, that all day long
Circled and soared and plunged on innocence; 'Cruel life,' I
    cried;
But my cry crossed over the woman's song,
Over the zither of the boat cutting the brine, and died,
And the man said, 'It is life,'
And the boat gritted the waiting sand
With sound of a cleansing knife,
And we slept, at life's command.

The Bomber

In a hollow of the forest
They were beyond neighbours;
He said to her, in a lift of peace
After their ecstasy—'Can it be?'
After a silence, when only the forest spoke,
He said, 'It is all roses,'

But she, more secretly listening,
Said, 'No! blue-cool cornflowers,'
But the forest, profound in nature's truth, said,
'No! It is lilies.'

There was a host about
Absorbed in secrecies,
Shut off and imprisoned in selves
Beyond good neighbourhood,
Beyond touch of friendliness,
Oneness, each separate,
Beyond dark, beyond light—
Insular insects in armour safe
Only pretending death;
Prisoned by fear.

There was no love about,
Neither in shape, sound, nor movement,
Only the protoplasm of love;
Thing ate thing, prowled and preyed,
In life foredoomed to dung;
But deaf, the man said,
'No! It is roses!'
She, with the ear of earth, said,
'It is blue-cool cornflowers.'
The forest said, 'It is
Funereal lilies!'

The lovers rose; pregnant with love,
Deaf to the moment, he cupped
A hand over her breast and they went
Home slowly in a sun
Descending over the purple hills;
The bomber roared over their dream.

A. D. HOPE

Australia

A nation of trees, drab green and desolate grey
In the field uniform of modern wars
Darkens her hills, those endless, outstretched paws
Of sphinx demolished or stone lion worn away.

They call her a young country, but they lie:
She is the last of lands, the emptiest,
A woman beyond her change of life, a breast
Still tender but within the womb is dry;

Without songs, architecture, history:
The emotions and superstitions of younger lands.
Her rivers of water drown among inland sands,
The river of her immense stupidity

Floods her monotonous tribes from Cairns to Perth.
In them at last the ultimate men arrive
Whose boast is not: 'we live' but 'we survive',
A type who will inhabit the dying earth.

And her five cities, like five teeming sores
Each drains her, a vast parasite robber-state
Where second-hand Europeans pullulate
Timidly on the edge of alien shores.

Yet there are some like me turn gladly home
From the lush jungle of modern thought, to find
The Arabian desert of the human mind,
Hoping, if still from the deserts the prophets come,

Such savage and scarlet as no green hills dare
Springs in that waste, some spirit which escapes
The learned doubt, the chatter of cultured apes
Which is called civilization over there.

Standardization

When, darkly brooding on this Modern Age,
The journalist with his marketable woes
Fills up once more the inevitable page
Of fatuous, flatulent, Sunday-paper prose;

Whenever the green aesthete starts to whoop
With horror at the house not made with hands
And when from vacuum cleaners and tinned soup
Another pure theosophist demands

Rebirth in other, less industrial stars,
Where huge towns thrust up in synthetic stone
And films and sleek miraculous motor-cars
And celluloid and rubber are unknown;

When, from his vegetable Sunday-school,
Emerges with the neatly maudlin phrase
Still one more Nature poet, to rant and drool
About the 'standardization of the race',

I see, stooping among her orchard trees,
The old, sound Earth, gathering her windfalls in,
Broad in the hams and stiffening at the knees,
Pause, and I see her grave, malicious grin.

For there is no manufacturer competes
With her in the mass production of shapes and things.
Over and over she gathers and repeats
The cast of a face, a million butterfly wings.

She does not tire of the pattern of a rose,
Her oldest tricks still catch us by surprise.
She cannot recall how long ago she chose
The streamlined hulls of fish, the snail's long eyes.

Love still pours into its ancient mould
The lashing seed that grows to a man again,
From whom by the same processes unfold
Unending generations of living men.

She has standardized his ultimate needs and pains;
Lost tribes in a lost language mutter in
His dreams; his science is tethered to their brains;
His guilt merely repeats Original Sin;

And beauty standing motionless before
Her mirror sees behind her, mile on mile,
A long queue in an unknown corridor,
Anonymous faces plastered with her smile.

RONALD McCUAIG

Betty by the Sea

Her drooping flowers dabble upon
Drooping breasts of crisp cretonne;
The thirsty sun has drained her breasts
Of milk of human interests

In babies, chatting, recipes,
Husband's pleasing lewderies
And gossip over the kitchen fence,
And left this earthy innocence;
The kindly sun has drained away
Her life, like suds on washing day,
And left her in this chair on the sands,
Clasping her flowers with laundered hands:
As though a storm of breeding-pains
And work and worry, which scoured her veins,
Had passed, she opens her tired eyes,
Like still seas, to vacant skies.

Love Me and Never Leave Me

Love me, and never leave me,
Love, nor ever deceive me,
And I shall always bless you
If I may undress you:
   Which I heard a lover say
   To his sweetheart where they lay.

He, though he did undress her,
Did not always bless her;
She, though she would not leave him,
Often did deceive him;
   Yet they loved, and when they died
   They were buried side by side.

Is Love Not Everlasting?

Is love not everlasting,
     And have I worn her lips away
With the hours' wasting,
     That their sweetness should decay
In the tasting?

O love's a sun still burning,
     And sweet as ever are her lips
For the shades yearning
     Of moving worlds to this eclipse
Not returning.

The Daily Round

The manager's desk revolves in business circles,
     Circled by desks in constant revolution,
Enveloped by the fetor of the workless
     The menace of whose painful destitution

Crawls through the house-phones saying 'Yes, sir'; 'No, sir';
     Or grates across a mile of city streets:
'I thought we'd get our order by September . . . ?'
     And the desk fountain-pen scrawls and repeats:

'J. Jones J. Jones J. Jones J. Jones J. Jones',
     Subscribing to his destiny: and plangent
Buzzers bar-off the conferential drones.
     The evening kicks him on his homing tangent.

JAMES PICOT

To the Rosella in the Poinsettia Tree

Beautiful bird, in as your wings as vivid
A tree, Rosella! Beautiful bird, I said:

'Your tent won't shelter you or love or me,
Red lad, these nine-o'-clocks, when Beauty looks
Pomp undue—indeed a ceremony
Too grand for the brown-eaten ribbed old livid
Wall behind of a tin factory!'

But the upward sun still burned them on
To tulip crimson from their poppy scarlet,
Those poinsettia petals, till at almost
Noon, he glowed in turn behind each moon,
Lamp, leaf,—the Wished-for-One—O, separate, crimson!—

For he seemed to burn each petal free,
Till but that Double Fire was to see—
And now there is but Light for Love to be!

Do You Not Hear?

Do you not hear
The answer of the year? Though pale,
Full-stamened, strong, the guava blows; the young
Persimmon is so like
His leaf, you must be near
To know he is already as big in the deep
Shadow his cradle as a young love-apple.
These things were made beautiful by sleep.

Finale

Forgive me, Lord, the callow things I say:
Thy pardon wants tomorrow as today.

We bruise the anvil for the iron-truth;
But in the morning when we go away
It is to live as though the knocks were vain;
And in the evening when we come again
It is the door we hammer for Thy ruth.

There is a jewel with Thy glory kissed
I have not fashioned in this random play.

Forgive me strangled heats and passion's mist:
Forgive me, Lord, tomorrow as today.

IAN MUDIE

Underground

Deep flows the flood,
deep under the land.
Dark is it, and blood
and eucalypt colour and scent it.
Deep flows the stream,
feeding the totem-roots,
deep through the time of dream
in Alcheringa.
Deep flows the river,
deep as our roots reach for it;

feeding us, angry and striving
against the blindness
ship-fed seas bring us
from colder waters.

REX INGAMELLS

Sea-chronicles

Where old-time ships came, canvas seagull-white,
articulate around our coast, the seas
speak sailors' Spanish, Dutch and Portuguese,
mutter and roar and whisper, day and night.

Lost names are sounded, could we hear aright,
that beat the Endeavour by two centuries
inside the Barrier Reef, and mysteries
resolved for which our scholars have no light.

Voices of water tell and tell and tell
the truths we cannot guess, and sun and stars
confirm and store the facts we have not found.

The winds know how a chill foreboding fell
upon a shore, where, jostled in by spars,
lay bodies of the first invaders, drowned.

WILLIAM HART-SMITH

When You Touch

When you touched the cold
rail that night, you said
My touch goes home along the
steel, all the way home.

Only a road and a railway-line,
for we were between stations,
and I said, Therefore the earth,
this common earth will do.

It is the same ground, and the whole
round world round the same
air you breathe, and I, and they;
and hand on heart

is hand on every heart.

Drama

Looking cautiously down they saw two men fishing,
Easing their lines above the snouts of the sharp rocks,
Advancing and retreating as the waves crashed green
And poured over their heavily-booted feet.

There was a square tank full to the brim with sea-water,
And a fire underneath where another squatted,
Tending it with sticks and sweet-smelling brushwood,
The breeze peeling a thin white vapour from the water,

And the watchers exchanged looks, and leant to look again,
Their round eyes taking in a complete drama and a complete
    picture,
Following the movements of the diminished figures,
And being hungry themselves were one body with the actors.

The tank was a new shape into their universe,
A new manipulation brought by these strangers;
And the fire beneath shot flames along its black belly.
The wind lifted a vapour from the water and silver droplets
    spun.

Fire is hot and water is cold, and water extinguishes fire;
But a sheet of iron is the secret of water brought to boiling.
The watchers, naked to the clean spring weather, come down
And merge into the picture that has only ourselves as onlookers
    now.

Curious, or deliberate theft, it does not matter:
One made to take a fish, and, plunging his arm to the elbow,
Received the full shock of the deadly West, and screamed.

Baiamai's Never-failing Stream

    Then he made of the stars, in my mind,
    pebbles and clear water running over them,
    linking most strangely feelings of im-
    measurable remoteness with intimacy,

    so that at one and the same time I
    not only saw a far white mist of stars
    there, far up there, but had my fingers
    dabbling among those cold stones.

Columbus Goes West

Columbus looks towards the New World,
The sea is flat and nothing breaks the rim
Of the world's disc;
He takes the sphere with him.

Day into night the same, the only change
The living variation at the core
Of this man's universe;
And silent on the silver ship he broods.

Red gouts of weed, and skimming fish, to crack
The stupefying emptiness of sea,
Night, and the unimpassioned gaze of stars . . .

And God be praised for the compass, oaths
Bawled in the fo'c'sle,
Broken heads, and wine,
Song and guitars,

The tramp of boots,
The wash and whip of brine.

Bathymeter

Those who have descended to the nethermost deeps
Of the ocean sealed in a bell
Past where the last blue-violet creeps

Imperceptibly away, and have hung
Suspended on a filament in utter dark,
While above them rung on rung

The colours of the spectrum ladder rise,
Say that the fish have lights
Like rows of portholes, dots around their eyes,

Headlamps of fluorescent studs,
Or lanterns hung on poles,
And the darkness is alive with moving buds

Of phosphorescence; fish with dim lit sails,
Shrimps that explode
In an enemy's face, and clouds of luminous snails.

And those who have been up in a balloon
So high the pale blue sky goes dark,
And darker, and the sun and moon

Burn pitilessly, say
The myriad stars appear
Shining at high noon of the brightest day.

In a liquid atmosphere that presses tight
With a multitude of tons,
Fish scrawl an aimless script direct in light;

While high above, a multitude of suns
In eternal night
Dance to a cosmic tune. And midway runs,

Precariously swung between extremes,
Our film of atmosphere, where light's diffused,
A narrow equipoise of pressure, heat and cold. It seems

This dance of stars in solemn time
And fish in swing is certain proof the Lord,
Whoever he be, cannot resist a rhyme.

ROLAND ROBINSON

Casuarina

The last, the long-haired casuarina
stands upon the hillside where,
against the turquoise night of those first
yellow stars, she shakes her hair.

She shakes her hair out in her singing
of cliffs and caves and waterfalls,
and tribes who left the lichened sandstone
carved in gods and animals.

This is her country: honeyeaters
cry out its aboriginal name
where on her ridges still the spear-tall
lilies burn in flame and flame.

I listen, and our legend says not
more than this dark singing tree,
although her golden flowering lover
lies slain beside the winter sea.

I Breathed into the Ash

I breathed into the ash,
I called upon the fire:
The hidden sleeping flower,
To waken and aspire.

I fed, with sheltering hand,
brush of the dead tea-tree
as incense rose between
the gums above the sea.

I breathe upon and bare
at flesh's, fibre's cost,
the spirit's coal unless
it darken and be lost,

be lost and never raise
its frankincense uncurled,
its clear flame from the ash,
the ruin of the world.

The Rock-lily's Pale Spray

The rock-lily's pale spray,
like sunlight, halts my way
up through the unpierced hush
of birdless blue-grey bush.
The rocks crouch on their knees
in earth, torsos of trees

and limb-boughs lead up where
the cliff-face scales the air.
Out from you, rock, my friend,
I lean and, reaching, bend
the scentless pale spray back
to me and see the black
spots in each orchid-flower.
O, my love, what power
keeps you curled and bound?
Tormented, the earth's round
begins again. What rock
holds you where you lock
yourself from me? Alone
this spray breaks from the stone.

ELIZABETH RIDDELL

News of a Baby

Welcome, baby, to the world of swords
And deadlier words.
We offer you a rough bed, and tears at morning,
And soon a playground
Bounded by ice and stones,
A buttonhole of thorns,
A kiss on war's corner.

We promise you, baby,
The stumble of fear in the heart,
The lurch of fear in the bones.

Painted upon your mother's cheek already
I see the dark effusion of your blood,
Bending already beside her patient chair the bandaged ghosts.

Welcome, baby, no dread thing will be omitted.
We are your eager hosts.

Country Tune

As I went out to walk
Beside the river flowing
I saw what I'd not hoped to see:
A black man washing a white horse.
That's how the world was going.

He washed the horse's tail
And plaited it with yellow.
The wild-west show had come to town.
That's how I saw the high white horse
And the brave black fellow.

The wild hawks flew above the smoke,
Above the river flowing;
The drunken cowboy stumbled past
And his long legs without his will
Took him where he was going.

I saw his eyes of bitter blue,
Who crossed my path unknowing,
Who would leap over my head that night
Over the tentpole, over the stars,
Over the river flowing.

I never hope to see again
The white horse decked in yellow,
The horse, the hawks, the river in flood,
The cowboy's eyes of bitter blue
Or the brave black fellow.

Forebears

I. *The Map*

O search the heart and belly you may find
The map of blood and it may have some meaning
But as for me as spring burns into summer and the blind
Suns follow each other to indifferent dark
I will embrace my other cousin, death,
Who long ago lay with my ancestors.

II. *The Reverend Edward Smith*

By Waggon Hill he went
Forgiving his parish,
His left and right neighbours,
His wife in her narrow bed
The sheets to her chin,
The keeper of the inn,
The cold man in the watch-house,
His cook and acquaintance,
Squire Rat in his high boots
And Lord and Lady Mouse.

But they not so lavish
With tender excuses
Refused to condone

His meagre black legs,
His long cold fingers,
The sighing of his prayers
On light bright mornings,
His hauntings and warnings.
And now he is dead
They avoid the stone
And the thin rim of grass
On his pious bone.

III. *John Teague*

He twined the country like a briar in the fair weather
But when the autumn gales
Tore at the stubborn roots of rocks and trees
Who lit his lamp?
For other men left home to live like saints or die like dogs
But he to practise divination.

The old women would pay him a penny to twitch
The bowels with fear
(Somewhat better than a witch
Because at least a man)
But the farmer would not hear
Ill omen of the harvest till it failed
And then they set the louts, the priests and fire,
The girls crying, and horses and men, the bishop in red
With hounds and prayer to run and read him out.

The village shuddered back into its dust
And he with blood about his head
Threaded the country like a briar,
But when the gales of autumn shook the world
Who lit his lamp?

He could endure the rods across his back
But not the woman and child beside the hearth.
He was John Teague
Who left his cobbler's shop
To practise divination.

IV. *Montfort Lee and Peter Cockerill*

When the ships *Nimbus* and *Pacific Fortune*
Slid under the southing star
To Hobart Town came I in the blood of Montfort Lee
And Peter Cockerill
(Of Bankbourne in this parish, deeply mourned)
Came I in their round pale eyes and pale smooth hair
And with them planted quinces, pears and wheat,
And with them rose at dawn to be a farmer,
And with them drank
(Gentry's white cuffs below the jacket sleeves)
Cider at Norfolk.
I was the seed they sowed when nothing stirred
Across the river but a kingfisher
Abreast of morning.
(Who laid the hopfields wide and planted vines,
And built a house of stone, and sailed a boat,
And went to marriages and funerals,
And matched each other's daughters with their sons,
And rode their horses by the willow-trees,
And seldom read a book or sang a song.)

V. *Mary Lomax*

Here is the woman with the face of pearl and rose,
The great madonna of misunderstanding, she
With laces at her wrist and the unearthly glow
Of ritual in her evening's arbour pose.

My mother's mother's mother, she in paint
And gilt by secondary artists set
Upon the wall. And all her axioms lie
As shattered mirrors round her, and the faint
Tinkle of teacups dies, and dies away.
Nothing is left of all she had to say.

VI. *The Man from Richmond*

The man from Richmond ran before
The lads upon his stumbling heel
Past the church and past the store,
Past the smith and the millwheel,
Past the rhododendrons drowned
Pale, pale, under the rain,
Ran, ran until he found
Shelter where the hawthorned lane
Turned to the meadow. There he lay,
Put his cheek to the earth and wept,
And cries of idiot died away,
And the man slept.
He the father, he the fool,
Caught between the hill and stream,
Between the cliff and the shallow pool,
The people and the dream.
He the zany, he the clod
Lying under the hawthorn-tree
Wept because he was not God.
He was I and I am he.

KEN BARRATT

Burke and Wills

I

So all men come at last to their Explorers' Tree,
Whereon they carve their valediction to the world.
Whether as they, we explore a continent, or are content
to explore ourselves, we find that mysterious centre,
that vast and utter loneliness, which is the heart of being;
we hear that silence more fatal than the siren's song.

II

Silence, like sound, has its eight note scale.
There is the silence after sound.
(After the farewell speeches, the well-wishings,
the cheering as they rode proudly from Melbourne Town,
the silence of the bush.)
There is the silence of sound we cannot hear.
(The black men, always lurking, always watching,
never speaking, merging in the frieze of great untidy trees.)
There is the silence amid many voices.
(Often they spoke loudly, hoping to drive their fears away,
hoping to fill the empty air with assurance,
but the silence was in them.)
There is the silence of Death, of the voice that can never be
        heard again.
(After Grey died, he seemed to march with them still,
the invisible companion, not answering their questions,
not questioning their answers.)
There is the silence of Desolation.
(This was no Egypt, but cresting a sand-dune,

they yet might discover the stones of a city, time-devoured,
or glinting in the sun, a golden helmet, become a hive
for the patient labour of the bees.)
There is the silence of Despair.
(Returning to the depot, finding it deserted,
they knew that words could buy them nothing
in this land of Nothing for Sale.)
There is the silence more ancient than man.
(Wills, the scientist, said it: *These rocks
are so old, they have forgotten the singing
and the shouting of the sea, the violence
of the earth in the making.*)
And last silence of all, completing the octave,
the silence that was before sound.
(Waiting for the end, life flowed backward to its source.
Voices, like a spring uncoiling,
receded and were superseded.
The last cry of hunger and pain
became the first cry for breath,
and now at last there was only the silence,
and they and the silence were one.)

III

Yet one man survived, one man returned
a little while to the world of men,
telling how Burke and Wills had died,
wresting the secret from a continent;
when they asked him to expound the secret,
he would speak of other things, saying rather,
'*The camels gave us trouble from the beginning,*'
or, '*Nardoo is no fit food for white men.*'

JOHN QUINN

A Foxhole for the Night

'Now I lay me down to sleep . . .'

Once if a man were dead and given to the earth
At least he'd sleep dry;
At least a coffin keeps the water out.

But this is a grave designed for the living,
Skilfully fashioned in the hot, red earth
and heaped with clotted soil about its edges.

Here, in his groundsheet shroud, a man can lie
Muffled in darkness, like a cocoon-swathed grub,
Until the rain-washed dawn
Comes with its weary bone-sore resurrection.

But the dawn is an unreality
Beyond an eternity of minutes.

The clumsy night is fidgeting with sound;
The running feet of the rain on the leaves,
The tired creaking of a dying tree,
The edged, violin whine of mosquitoes.

And water reaches down these walls of earth
And twists warm, flowing fingers
Indecently through sodden clothes.

The consciousness of earth
And an unwashed body
Is a sick taste in the mouth
And a thickness in the throat.

155

And time can end with a movement in the vines.
A grenade's iron voice will tell of the ending
Or the tongue of a knife will whisper it.

'Gentle Jesus, meek and mild,
Look upon a little child.'

DOUGLAS STEWART

Old Iron

There are no instructions here for that dazzling man,
So frail in front of the engine, who one fine day
Will leap to the track and switch the points, they say,
And save the time from disaster, set the great wheels
Roaring at last on the true, the only way;

No more than a lump of iron for that man to look at
As I am looking while the crabs scuttle and hide
And the backs of the limpets dry as the seaweed has dried
To the stillness of stone, and the wrack cast up by the sea
Rusts in the sun and awaits the returning tide.

One of those weathered and very mad old men
Who live alone in their humpies, outlaws alike
From the holiday crowds who snatch at the waves and shriek
Like gulls at a meatworks, and whatever goal or disaster
Or mere receding distance our time will strike,

One of those withered and very mad old men
Concerned with their own slow rusting in natural leisure
Should be here with me, is here in my mind to treasure
This twisted bit of a ship, this battered junk,
And stretch his hand to the iron with a cry of pleasure,

Though nobody else, unless some wandering boy,
Is likely to spare it a glance. If a dumb yearning
Calls iron, after the hammering and the burning,
Back to its native earth, this has its wish:
Seabird and fish accept it as rock returning,

And as flesh and bone of the earth it takes the sun
And glows with life, or receives the sea and crumbles.
And now as always when the mind's old madman stumbles
On some such rock, and pauses, and fills with light
At an apparition of Earth, his hand trembles

And stretches out to the simple touch of the iron
As towards another hand, or to warm spring air,
Water or tree or stone, in a gesture of prayer
And sweet communion with things that accept in peace
The rhythms of earth beyond our control or care.

Lava on Egmont, shellrock at Mangamingi,
There were always sacred rocks and sacred trees,
And beside the breakwater cutting the violent seas
At far New Plymouth like a searchlight thrust in a storm,
A gigantic rusty anchor took its ease;

And far away back into childhood at Opunake
Was a shaft of iron in a rock, so deeply thrust
No giant could shake it though spray had flaked it with rust;
And no one could tell us why it was driven there
By the old mysterious men, themselves now dust.

What shall we say, old madman, of this old iron,
Meteorite on a lonely Australian reef
From the age's whirling planet of hope and grief?
Iron that stands like the earth's accusing ghost
In city buildings, iron that without relief

Roars on the rails of the world, both track and engine
For the whole adventure and drive of the urgent mind,
Lies calmly here, forgetting tormented mankind
In the older life of the earth where the simple creatures
Obey their natures and the rock is dumb and blind.

And likely enough, one of those mad old men
Will creep from his hole when the age has crashed at last
And stare at the wreck of iron and mutter aghast
'So the blind rush came to this; the earth has got them.'
But the old man hides in a hole; we thunder past,

Committed to high adventure, and what we have seen
Who cannot see our far-off stopping place,
Of the life of the earth glowing or crumbling in grace,
Is half a meeting in joy and half a goodbye,
Like seeing in the rain at night a woman's face.

Terra Australis

Captain Quiros and Mr William Lane,
Sailing some highway shunned by trading traffic
Where in the world's skull like a moonlit brain
Flashing and crinkling rolls the vast Pacific,

Approached each other zigzag, in confusion,
Lane from the west, the Spaniard from the east,
Their flickering canvas breaking the horizon
That shuts the dead off in a wall of mist.

'Three hundred years since I set out from Lima
And off Espiritu Santo lay down and wept
Because no faith in men, no truth in islands,
And still unfound the shining continent slept;

'And swore upon the Cross to come again
Though fever, thirst and mutiny stalked the seas
And poison spiders spun their webs in Spain,
And did return, and sailed three centuries,

'Staring to see the golden headlands wade
And saw no sun, no land, but this wide circle
Where moonlight clots the waves with coils of weed
And hangs like silver moss on sail and tackle,

'Until I thought to trudge till time was done
With all except my purpose run to waste;
And now upon this ocean of the moon,
A shape, a shade, a ship, and from the west!'

II

'What ship?' 'The Royal Tar!' 'And whither bent?'
'I seek the new Australia.' 'I, too, stranger;
Terra Australis, the great continent
That I have sought three centuries and longer;

'And westward still it lies, God knows how far,
Like a great golden cloud, unknown, untouched,
Where men shall walk at last like spirits of fire
No more by oppression chained, by sin besmirched.'

'Westward there lies a desert where the crow
Feeds upon poor men's hearts and picks their eyes;
Eastward we flee from all that wrath and woe
And Paraguay shall yet be Paradise.'

'Eastward,' said Quiros, as San Pedro rolled,
High-pooped and round in the belly like a barrel,
'Men tear each other's entrails out for gold;
And even here I find that men will quarrel.'

'If you are Captain Quiros you are dead.'
'The report has reached me; so is William Lane.'
The dark ships rocked together in the weed
And Quiros stroked the beard upon his chin:

'We two have run this ocean through a sieve
And though our death is scarce to be believed
Seagulls and flying-fish were all it gave
And it may be we both have been deceived.'

III

'Alas, alas, I do remember now;
In Paradise I built a house of mud
And there were fools who could not milk a cow
And idle men who would not though they could.

'There were two hundred brothers sailed this ocean
To build a New Australia in the east
And trifles of money caused the first commotion
And one small cask of liquor caused the last.

'Some had strange insects bite them, some had lust,
For wifeless men will turn to native women,
Yet who could think a world would fall in dust
And old age dream of smoke and blood and cannon

'Because three men got drunk?' 'With Indian blood
And Spanish hate that jungle reeked to Heaven;
And yet I too came once, or thought I did,
To Terra Australis, my dear western haven,

'And broke my gallows up in scorn of violence,
Gave land and honours, each man had his wish,
Flew saints upon the rigging, played the clarions:
Yet many there were poisoned by a fish

'And more by doubt, and so deserted Torres
And sailed, my seamen's prisoner, back to Spain.
There was a certain likeness in the stories
And Captain Quiros stared at William Lane.

IV

Then, 'Hoist the mainsail!' both the voyagers cried,
Recoiling each from each as from the devil;
'How do we know that we are truly dead
Or that the tales we tell may not be fable?

'Surely I only dreamed that one small bottle
Could blow up New Australia like a bomb?
A mutinous pilot I forbore to throttle
From Terra Australis send me demented home?

'The devil throws me up this Captain Quiros,
This William Lane, a phantom not yet born,
This Captain Quiros dead three hundred years,
To tempt me to disaster for his scorn—

'As if a blast of bony breath could wither
The trees and fountains shining in my mind,
Some traveller's tale, puffed out in moonlit weather,
Divert me from the land that I must find!

'Somewhere on earth that land of love and faith
In Labor's hands—the Virgin's—must exist,
And cannot lie behind, for there is death,
So where but in the west—but in the east?'

At that the sea of light began to dance
And plunged in sparkling brine each giddy brain;
The wind from Heaven blew both ways at once
And west went Captain Quiros, east went Lane.

M   161

The Sunflowers

'Bring me a long sharp knife for we are in danger;
I see a tall man standing in the foggy corn
And his high, shadowy companions.'—'But that is no stranger,
That is your company of sunflowers; and at night they turn
Their dark heads crowned with gold to the earth and the dew
So that indeed at daybreak, shrouded and silent,
Filled with a quietness such as we never knew,
They look like invaders down from another planet.
And now at the touch of light from the sun they love'—
'Give me the knife. They move.'

Helmet Orchid

Oh such a tiny colony
Set amongst all eternity
Where the great bloodwoods stand!
It is the helmet orchid
That will not lift itself
Higher than a fallen leaf
But waits intent and secret
Leaning its ear to the ground.

What could it hear but silence?
Yet where the orchid listens
Low in its purple hood
Among the trees' immensity,
Out of the depth of the world
Dark and rainy and wild
Sounding through all eternity
Silence like music flowed.

EVE LANGLEY

Native-born

In a white gully among fungus red
  Where serpent logs lay hissing at the air,
I found a kangaroo. Tall, dewy, dead,
So like a woman, she lay silent there.
Her ivory hands, black-nailed, crossed on her breast,
  Her skin of sun and moon hues, fallen cold.
Her brown eyes lay like rivers come to rest
  And death had made her black mouth harsh and old.
Beside her in the ashes I sat deep
  And mourned for her, but had no native song
To flatter death, while down the ploughlands steep
  Dark young Camelli whistled loud and long,
'Love, liberty, and Italy are all.'
  Broad golden was his breast against the sun.
I saw his wattle whip rise high and fall
  Across the slim mare's flanks, and one by one
She drew the furrows after her as he
  Flapped like a gull behind her, climbing high,
Chanting his oaths and lashing soundingly,
  While from the mare came once a blowing sigh.
The dew upon the kangaroo's white side
  Had melted. Time was whirling high around,
Like the thin wommera, and from heaven wide
  He, the bull-roarer, made continuous sound.
Incarnate lay my country by my hand:
  Her long hot days, bushfires, and speaking rains,
Her mornings of opal and the copper band
  Of smoke around the sunlight on the plains.

Globed in fire-bodies the meat-ants ran
  To taste her flesh and linked us as we lay,
For ever Australian, listening to a man
  From careless Italy, swearing at our day.
When, golden-lipped, the eagle-hawks came down
  Hissing and whistling to eat of lovely her,
And the blowflies with their shields of purple brown
  Plied hatching to and fro across her fur,
I burnt her with the logs, and stood all day
  Among the ashes, pressing home the flame
Till woman, logs, and dreams were scorched away,
  And native with night, that land from whence they came.

Australia

The brown round of the continent tonight
Rises up, shoulder on shoulder, searching for the sun;
And all the white French rains that once took flight
Into the earth, rise slowly, one by one,
Remembering Villon who left a rag on every tree.
Perhaps he walked Australia long ago,
Mourning for all those women white and sad as snow.
Verlaine perhaps enchanted by our seas
Cried in his lyric voice that purple hours
Lay waxen-mitred in our purple flowers . . .
The wildflowers of Australia; a thin brown
Veil of lost Autumn is somehow caught around
Their stalks unspeaking, as though Springtime at the core
Was a small child lost in the bush for ever more.

This Year, Before It Ends

This year, before it ends, holds out time as a weight to us,
We that are met in the streets as the streets are met in us,
And light is a weight, too; men shake it mightily off.
A youth, kicking the self-starter of a motor-bike, sends
A vast vibration out to the sun, and it returns his shadow in
    rain.
Out from the sun startles the line of things, and the flying cars
Set their undertones in a dark and silver note upon the line.
Even the weeds, ground weeds, can in their green brains sing
    that song.
This year, before it ends, is the imploring city—ageing before
    us.
Raising the delicate dust from the streets as a veil that will
Set million-branched forests sibilant before its eyes . . . Faint
    darkness,
And the desolate set of the tides, hidden: only the shadowed
    face
Dust-powdered, stone-calm, set to us, and the sad cry of the
    pilgrims
In the slow patch of moonlight under the nameless trees,
    crying
'Our god was night-hour, and the white path before us;
We, the homeless; and the shuddering branches ours and the
    great moan,
Rising out of agony, and the going, form on form of the dead;
And the façade that we are; this year before it ends.'

KENNETH MACKENZIE

Confession

All I have got of wealth and wisdom, I
   have spent too hungrily on wine and men,
fearing that some tomorrow I should die
   rich, wise and loveless, into dust again,
my laughter never loosed, my tears unshed,
   cold, virtuous corpse stretched on a feather bed.

This spendthrift hunger, whetted on this fear,
   bullied its bread, ate like a famished beast
in watchful rage, and never did forbear,
   but snatched at every platter of the feast—
love, hatred, friendship, charity,
   malice and kindness—all were one to me.

I lived full selfishly while time allowed,
   cast conscience out, invited in despair,
lay down with joy, walked lonely with the crowd,
   read, wrote and ravished all I thought was fair,
kept much, and lost the much I could not keep,
and found, like others, life's best bliss was sleep.

So now, sprawled dead upon the plain of Time,
   churned by the worms of living memories,
I see I have been wise to feel no crime
   in spending all on these eternities
of men and wine, to buy on earth a heaven
Such as to better men was never given.

Caesura

Sometimes at night when the heart stumbles and stops
a full second endless the endless steps
that lead me on through this time terrain
without edges and beautiful terrible
are gone never to proceed again.

Here is a moment of enormous trouble
when the kaleidoscope sets unalterable
and at once without meaning without motion
like a stalled aeroplane in the middle sky
ready to fall down into a waiting ocean.

Blackness rises. Am I now to die
and feel the steps no more and not see day
break out its answering smile of hail all's well
from east full round to east and hear the bird
whistle all creatures that on earth do dwell?

Not now. Old heart has stopped to think of a word
as someone in a dream by far too weird
to be unlikely feels a kiss and stops
to praise all heaven stumbling in all his senses . . .
and suddenly hears again the endless steps.

The Snake

Withdrawing from the amorous grasses
from the warm and luscious water
the snake is soul untouched by both
nor does the fire of day through which it passes
mark it or cling. Immaculate navigator
it carries death within its mouth.

Soul is the snake that moves at will
through all the nets of circumstance
like the wind that nothing stops,
immortal movement in a world held still
by rigid anchors of intent or chance
and ropes of fear and stays of hopes.

It is the source of all dispassion
the voiceless life above communion
secret as the spring of wind
nor does it know the shames of self-confession
the weakness that enjoys love's coarse dominion
or the betrayals of the mind.

Soul is the snake the cool viator
sprung from a shadow on the grass
quick and intractable as breath
gone as it came like the everlasting water
reflecting God in immeasurable space—
and in its mouth it carries death.

Legerdemain

Ah me the hand upon the body
  the whorled speech
that sings from fingertips a wordless melody
  mounting with the delicate increasing touch
  to a long cry in the mind can never reach
  the end of the search.

Night has a thousand I O U's
  signed with sighs
shaken out of the blood that floods imperious
  the flesh touched delicately and by day these
  flutter unhonoured along habitual byways
  past averted eyes.

Or perhaps one that said *tomorrow*
  is redeemed
by accident on the stair or in the mirror
  where eyes look curiously into eyes doomed
  for ever to look back curiously or dimmed
  by what they dreamed.

For not eyes but hands only can see
  in night's alley
that leads from nowhere nowhere and keeps busy
  the shuddering direction-finder love's ally
  pointing a staggering track to melancholy
  through heaven's valley.

Ah me the seeing skin reports
 certain replies
signalling a hasty offering of transports
 and through the dark viaduct the eyeless music plays
 with drums diminishing and frantic pleas
 keep moving please.

The hand upon the body dies instead
 of reason dying
though for some moments consciousness insisted
 reason had died in the divine undoing
 of ties with earth.
      Sense now steadying
hears spirit crying.

JOHN BLIGHT

Becalmed

Above and below the ship, this blue:
No cloud, no island, and which of two
Suns was celestial, submarine?
Each sailor shrugged. Who'd ever been
South of the Line . . . who knew . . . who knew?

There was a vessel in the sky—
Towering above, or below the eye?
If only something would drift past,
Seaweed or cloud to foul its mast.
Why should it, too, becalmed thus, lie?

Below and above, the seeming sea
Like a great eye which dreamily
Sees nothing, and by nothing is seen;
A waking that may, may not, have been.
'Which of us now is you, is me?'

Everything double under the sun;
And doubly doubled to prove which one
Is under which, which sun above.
'God, if the counterpart would move.'
But the movement there or here is none.

'Silver's a man is full of cunning;
Monkey, he is on the taffrail running;
Agile, he props and dives right in.
One rises to meet him with a grin.
Head strikes head with a smack that's stunning.

'No more Silver, he's under the sea;
Or up in the sky, or where is he?'
Lost in the ether, south of the Line;
The eight bells rang, but we heard nine:
And where are we, and where are we?

Lord, it is dark. The two suns met
In a blaze of flame we won't forget:
And which ate which, we could not say;
But night came on and at close of day
We cheered. 'All's not proved double yet.'

Too soon, too soon! The moon that rose
Split into two, like silver shoes:
One walked the sky, one walked the sea;
But which walked which was strange to me:
For south of the Line, who knows . . . who knows?

'This is the other half,' I said.
'Since Egypt, here they've buried the dead,
Under the earth and south of the Line.'
The eight bells rang and we heard nine.
'We are they whom the mermaids wed.'

Doomed on a ship that is dead, becalmed;
In a winding sheet of blue, embalmed.
'Friend, it is doubly strange I feel,
No-one will credit our plight was real;
We dead, in a ship that is dead, becalmed.'

The Cat-o'-Nine-Tails

Given the 'Cat', it was not only that he ran
A gauntlet of whips—one could bear that
Before the mast in a salt gale—but a man
Could not rally at those words, 'Convict rat'.

The delirious Cat striking with its nine
Tails, vigour and abandon of nine lives,
Mauling him, 'Convict rat'. How refine
Punishment with humour better with knives?

Cheap gibe, the Cat. It sprang again, again;
And pain filled in the hollows between ribs.
'Give him the Cat,' said voices in his brain;
'Convict rat . . . we'll break his blasted nibs.'

'Cat . . . Cat . . . give him the Cat.' He remembered
Sentence and pretence of humour grim:
And, when he felt through torture one dismembered,
Down from the triangle they bundled him.

What niceties of morning between bars
Matched his red scars; what sun's salve
Mended his hide? Better if scimitars
Descend now to quarter or halve

His striped agony—striped like a cat.
That humour would intrude. He rallied now. . . .
Milady's kitten? How he grinned at that,
Grimaces that would make one wonder how

Solace was in this as the kitten came—
'It would have done this deed; remember that,
Convict rat. It would have done the same!'
He fondled with steeled heart Milady's cat.

Crab

Shellfish and octopus, and all the insane
Thinking of the undersea, to us is lost.
At most is food, in our higher plane.
But, what of this submarine ghost—
Life, without its meddling monkey? Can
The crab regenerate into prototype merman?
Sea, of nightmare pressure and mask—
Green faces in the gloom—what is your task
In creation; or is it over? Has space
Such aquariums of planets trapped? Was
Eden thus? Oh, pressures which the lace
Sponge of the brain survives. What has
The life of the sea of my ignorance,
But such creatures; much of this wild-shaped chance!

Stonefish and Starfish

These are the first shapes: stonefish and starfish.
Imagine the stone falling, tumbling down the scree
Through the upper atmosphere. Here you may wish
To see a stone move, too; but the cobbles under the sea
Stare patently—dead pupils. Oh, roll a cobble
To life, even such lowly life, till it swims like a bubble . . .
I looked longing, too, into the lonely deeps
But knew I watched ages after the first star.
If I could will life there, raise it by steps
To perfection, it would be as we are.
Starfish, I know you, now, staring as I have
Where a star would long gaze for its image to move. . . .
These are the first shapes, life in its first steps.
See, now, man gazes into the outer deeps.

HAROLD STEWART

Dialogue of the Way
(for C. T. Brown)

Wu Tao-tzŭ, the greatest of Chinese painters.
Hui Nêng, the Sixth Patriarch of Ch'an Buddhism.

Earliest spring, and clouds at dawn are few.
The rising sky is sharp and chilly blue,
Clear as a sapphire, where an upward glow
Lights the eastern horizon from below.
Like prunus-blossom floating on the floes
Of cracking river-ice, the clouds dispose
Petals thereon, incomparably white,
Which dawn has filled with crisp, silver light.

Now bubbles grain the ice, and frigid rivers
Shake their backs and fracture into shivers.
Now the watered ice-sheet rapidly breaks
Up into jagged and congested cakes.
Streams are released and eastward start to flow,
A frozen slush, at first, with mud and snow;
Till free their sparkling sapphire waters gush
And heave their jostling splinters in their rush
A crystal wreckage high along the shore.
The last wild storm of winter stripped and tore
Clouds of white prunus-blossom: here they strew
The ice, a crackled field of deeper blue.

And while the China sky receives a glaze
Of azure, on this first of fresh spring days,
The painter and the patriarch prepare
To set out from the mountain temple, where
They have found lodging all the winter through.
Wu is amused but puzzled, as they do,
By Hui Nêng, whose composite attire
Prompts his curiosity to enquire:

Wu Tao-tzŭ

'Now, Master Hui Nêng, what are you at?
I see you have assumed the formal hat
Of an orthodox Confucian; yet you wear
The robe of Buddha's followers, and bear
A staff for pilgrimage; you even use,
To end this odd assortment, Taoist shoes!
Why are you dressed in all of these together?'

Hui Nêng

'The hat protects my head in rainy weather;
The robe gives warmth against a freezing day;
The staff and shoes support me on my way.
And mind you now, I mean but what I say:
I don't indulge in myth or metaphor!'

Wu Tao-tzŭ

'I am no wiser than I was before.
But since you are enlightened, tell me, sir:
When from the Eightfold Path my footsteps err,
How shall I follow it with faltering tread?'

Hui Nêng

'Oh, just keep on walking straight ahead.'

But Wu is troubled as to what is meant,
And silent, as they start on their descent.
Already on the slopes the snow had thinned
When, last night, a rough but humid wind
Blew up the fog, blew up the tepid rain
That melt the snowbanks down to earth again;
And honeycomb the smoothly moulded shapes
And domes of snow, which trickles and escapes.
The mounds of glass in liquefaction wane,
As warmer waters in the flooded lakes
Dissolve away the final icy flakes:
Signs that the thaw's revolt has overthrown
The dynasty of frost, to found its own.

Wu Tao-tzŭ

'You tell me that you use no sleight of speech,
And yet your words are wild; they do not teach
But tease me with a meaning out of reach.
Enough of these evasions. Show me now
In what direction I must follow Tao.'

Hui Nêng

'The hills and valleys at this time of year
When winter thaws, and spring is almost freed,
Invite you to explore them. There are here
No crossroads and no by-ways to mislead;
Nor are there walls or ditches that might baulk
Your legs from taking some delightful walk.
You need no map or guide to find your way.
Follow your nose: you cannot go astray,
No matter what direction, east or west.'

Wu Tao-tzŭ

'You mean to put my patience to the test;
But I will make you yield your secret yet.
Where lies the Middle Way?'

Hui Nêng

        'Your feet are set
Upon it here and now. Before your eyes
The pathway trodden by the Buddha lies.
Does language still obscure it from your sight?
Put your left foot forward, then your right!'

Exasperated by the monk's absurd
Instruction, Wu proceeds without a word.

The ridges have grown balder overnight,
With isles of russet in their seas of white.
The land is left as chequered as the bark
Of bare white-poplars, where it splits to mark
Their silver limbs with diamonds of dark.
And half-exposed recline the lower hills,
Lyrical with a choir of little rills
That seek the sea with music through the plains,
Carrying off the winter in their veins;
Whose silver tributaries lace the land
Like veins branching in a poplar's hand.
The day approaching now with radiant beam,
Vapours exhale, and all the valleys steam.
Here is a world in deliquescence, where
Tongues of evaporation lick the air;
And on all sides is heard the sinking sound,
Faint but distinct, uttered by drinking ground.

J. P. McAULEY

The Blue Horses

(In honour of Franz Marc)

I

What loud wave-motioned hooves awaken
Our dream-fast members from the cramp of sleep?
The tribal images are shaken
And crash upon their guardians. The skies
Are shivered like a pane of glass.

Progeny of winds, sea-forms, earth-bestriders
From the blue quarries of their natal hills

Terribly emerging to their riders,
Blue Horses lift their neighing trumpets to the moon!
They stamp among the spiritual mills
That weave a universe from our decay:
The specious outline crumbles at the shock
Of visionary hooves, and in dismay
Men hide among the tumbled images.

The silver trumpets strike the moon!
O grasp the mane with virgin hand:
Beneath the knocking of the magic hoof
New spaces open and expand.
For in the world are spaces infinite
And each point is a mighty room
Where flowers with strange faces bloom
In the amazing light;
And every little crystal minute
Has many aeons locked within it
Within whose crystal depths we see
Times upon times eternally.

II

The whittled moon
Lies on the steep incline of night
Flanked by a stair of fading stars.
The hooves are silent.
Chimney-stacks
Pour their first smoke-trail across
The lightening cloud-bars.
The first wheel clacks
On grinding gears,
The pulley whirrs upon its boss.

Naked you lie and your own silence keep,
The arms of love are laid aside in sleep.
Soon it will be day like other days:
I cannot hold this hour in my hand
Nor press
Its image on a substance beyond time.
Possess!
But we are never in possession
And nothing stays at our command.
Possess!
Yet day comes on.
The delicate steel cranes manoeuvre
Like giant birds above their load;
The high song of the tyres is heard
Along the whitening road.
Possess!
All things escape us, as we too escape.
We have owned nothing and have no address
Save in the poor constriction
Of a legal or poetic fiction.
He that possesses is possessed
And falsifies perception lest
The visionary hooves break through
The simple seeming world he knew.
Possess!
His wife hangs lace across the view
And all they know of lucid lithe Septembers
Is guilty dreams and itching members.

The harbour derricks swing their load upon the shore.
The sacred turbines hum, the factories
Set up their hallowed roar.

Men must awake betimes and work betimes
To furnish the supplies of war.
For some shall work and some possess
And all shall read the morning papers
And from the world's ripped entrails there displayed
Haruspicate the trends of love and trade.

Sleep no more, for while you sleep
Our love is stolen by the cheating sun
And angry frightened men destroy
Our peace with diktat, pact, and gun.
The old men of the tribe go mad
And guard with malice, fraud and guile
The sacred enzymes of a world gone bad.
The hoof-beats thunder in my ears.
Leave to the councillors the garbage-plot,
The refuse and the greasy tins
Of this slum-culture—these are not
The area where love begins.
The brutal and the vile are set
As watchers at the gate,
But the Blue Horses scream aloud:
A sudden movement shakes the crowd
Stampeded on the hooves of fate.

New Guinea Lament

Now glowing Venus wakes
On the tumulus of dusk
And the roaming wild-pig shakes
The dead with rooting tusk.

The flying-foxes swarm
In fading orchards of light,
The keeper cannot keep from harm
Fruit stolen in the night.

My love now are you lying
In the mirrors of your sleep
Or do you watch with inward sighing
Earth's hungry shadows creep

On the dreary day's remains?
Desire like a rusty nail
Pierces time's foot until it seems
His aching tread will fail.

Missa Papae Marcelli

Now Ixion's wheel is stilled
By that pure rejoicing tone;
Sisyphus the adverse-willed
Sits in quiet by his stone;
For in hell, when music sounds,
Spirits leave their barren rounds.

Sexes that were damned in sin
Outwards turn their quenchless eyes
That before were fixed within
On their gnawing miseries;
When music sounds, the glances meet
Gently, and forgo deceit.

Rulers, artists, who were spent
By ambition that proved vain,
Shake the eternal discontent
From their shoulders; and the pain
Ceases to assault its bounds,
Regenerate, when music sounds.

Sabbath on the brows of Dis!
Earth is silent as a bride.
The shining calm parenthesis
Stills the angry worlds outside.
Magog, looming at the gate,
When music sounds, forgets his hate.

The Death of Chiron

The herdboys shout unseen among the rocks;
Autumn grows colder, and they lead their flocks
From the high pastures down into the plain.
To feel the golden calm I have dragged my pain
Outside the cavern mouth, but still inhale
The smell of sweat and sickness, dung and stale.

The wild bees know the time of dearth has come,
And signal the grim rites of harvest-home
When crumpled bodies of the drones are thrust
Out of the hive and fall into the dust.
The year sinks underground, and with it I
Put off divinity and learn to die.

A son of Time no less than Zeus, I chose
To be the friend of centaurs and all those
Who draw a harsh life from this mountain breast.

I tutored many heroes, but loved best
The hardy unheroic simple folk
Who drive their herds and put the ox to yoke.

I taught them spells and simples that could salve
Their peaceful wounds, or help their cows to calve;
Even the village girls would come for charms
To guard against lost love or freckled arms,
Leaving small gifts of honey, eggs, or fruit;
Or sometimes, laughing, would not long dispute

Among the crushed herbs of the cave to measure
What god and beast can bring to country pleasure.
Sometimes in the spring I joined the dance
With hard hooves beating, and the men would prance
In mimic masks to lead the season in;
And what was done those nights was not held sin.

In winter when the owl sat humped with cold
I came down to their firesides and told
Stories of gods and heroes; and often then
Would tell of one who brought down fire to men,
And how, before the Hero sets him free,
Some god must give his immortality

And die: not as the sacred ear of corn
Lies in darkness waiting to be reborn,
But as the dry stalk falls and vanishes.
A dear exchange it seemed—nor did I guess
What hydra-poisoned arrow, from what bow,
Would send me willing to the shades below.

Heracles, saviour of men, sun-like defender,
I watched your youth rise to its noon-splendour
Of clear heroic fire; but feared to see
The fitful presage of that insanity,
When blundering in a dark eclipse you strike
At shadows, killing friend and child alike.

So Linus died, and Eunomus, then all
Your children; and the darkness yet will fall
On others, as it did on me that day
When the odorous wine-cask bred the wild affray
That drove the routed centaurs to my cave;
And I went down to stay your hand and save

The hunted. I saw blind frenzy in your soul
Like shadows wavering in a red-hot coal,
Such as the warriors of Asia feel
But quench their bodies, as men temper steel,
Hissing in the wave. Unchecked you drew
The bowstring taut, and the long arrow flew.

As the devising wasp with darting skill
Thrusts in her sting to paralyse, not kill,
The insect that survives to be the prey
Of her hatched grub when she has flown away,
So did attentive Fate spring forth to guide
The venomed stroke, then vanish satisfied.

Now when the shepherds bring their summer flocks
To the high pasture-ground among the rocks,
They are afraid to come near where I lie.
There is no herb or spell can purify
The inherent hydra; why should I not consent
To free the Titan from his banishment?

Never was earth more radiant than in this
Last autumn gold that I take down to Dis.
I have loved the earth alone, and had no will
To change the measures of its good and ill;
Others give laws and blame, and sit above,
But there were no conditions in my love.

Men will bewail my fate when I am gone
And in it see the pattern of their own:
Their poisoned instinct writhes incurable
Within the ancient cave of touch and smell;
They feel the hydra-taint of guilty care
Rankle their joy and bring them to despair.

But in exchange, instead of plaited straw,
The heavy golden crown of art and law
Will press upon their brows, and in their hand
The imperial builder's dream of stone will stand;
And on the rustic year they will impose
New time, that does not vary as it flows.

Yet their Promethean victories will rise
But as the smoke of nature's sacrifice
Within, without. Everywhere they tread
The beasts will sicken and the desert spread.
Their baffled Hero in his turn will die
Howling in envenomed agony.

I have but little skill of forward sight,
Nor have I overheard in the still night,
As once the Titan did, the singing Fates:
The spirit alone can judge what it creates
And see it to the end. But I must go
Unreconciled into the dark below.

ERIC IRVIN

Midnight Patrol

Now as the night treads softly on its way,
And trees review the march-past of the stars,
We stand and hear leaves chatter. Do they say:
'These must be, surely, visitors from Mars?'
For death is cradled in my arms, my belt
Holds bitter fruit for enemies to eat;
While at my back, four aces yet undealt,
Tread riflemen with slow and wary feet.
Tall trees spring from the darknesses that lie
About their base to greet the moon, but we
Shrink from her light for fear the unseen eye
Should mark our shapes merged with a light-splashed tree
And free the lightning that would make us one
With night that never sees a rising sun.

Brother Ass

Old Brother Ass stands mumchance in the sun,
Dreaming the century's dream of easy wealth,
Dreaming the golden prize; then thumbs in stealth
The latest ticket. In his mind this dun,
Black-printed rag hangs gracefully across
Uneven doorways, shutting out the black
Worm-eaten timbers of the past. Its folds
Are tapestried in gold utopian scenes
Wherein the world is his, or not, for toss
Of any coin from out a well-filled sack.

He folds it up. Tomorrow's drawing holds
So much of his real life within its hands
He dare not think an instant more on fate,
Whose end he neither sees nor understands.

Old Brother Ass stands mumchance in the sun
(The years have taught him only how to wait),
Confined within the glasshouse of his means;
Seeing the world outside with eyes that shun
The greater glasshouse round his smaller one.

Christmas 1942

I

Here's shade and comfort by this towering tree,
Dear Phaedrus, and a breeze to lull our rest.
Here let our thoughts flow undisturbed and free
As flows Laloki. Many sands have run
Since by Ilissus you and I reclined;
And many comrades journeyed to the sun
With whom we have shared everything but death.

II

I could not speak of them on my return;
I could not bare the wound so closely wrapped
Against corruption by the spoken word;
My smile the dreamer's shield held up to guard
A sense of impotence, a deep despair
Of making 'over here' see 'over there'.

But someone spoke of Damas and Djezzine,
And phrased a pretty speech about Tobruk,
And in a flash the cramped suburban room,
The silly teacups and the linen cloth,
The heartless sympathy of common speech
Moved out beyond the compass of Time's reach:

And I was in a man's world, and the earth
Shook or stood still as we chose to dictate;
And life was ours, and death, and the sweet pain
Of thinking now and then of other days
When we were human beings, sheltered, fed;
The darlings of existence, fancy-led.

III

Bitterness sways me but a while: is gone,
And I remember mornings such as this
By such a green-banked, slowly-flowing stream
An aeon of experience ago.
Remember, too, a love that down the years
Has mocked me with its echoed might-have-been.

These notes I gather now; all chords resolve
In pointed harmony phrased by despair;
New-cadenced by regrets that rise and fall;
That hint of a solemn pity: and are gone.

EDGAR HOLT

Two Sonnets from a Sequence

I

This side of madness, while the flames abate,
They have heaped their small belongings: tears
(Harsh in pain-dry eyes), hunger and hate,
And all their monstrous catalogue of fears.
Death is the least of these—a troubled sleep
Invaded by the memory of pain,
So much, that even those who die still weep,
And bones cry out and sinews are insane.

At night the children dream, clutching the air
With knotted hands. . . . O sweet to dream of hell,
Where fallen angels burn! O sweet to stare,
Sleepbound, on demons! . . . No, their nightmares tell
The day's tale over, and they run from men,
They run, they run, until they wake again.

II

Under the midnight's iron rain, under
The ground, under the broken wall and arch,
And the fallen city, there's no room for wonder.
Love is a moment stolen from the march—
The other side of killing, lust that cleaves,
A dry fulfilment of despair, the splinter
Piercing the heart. Its bitter warmth deceives
As cruelly as a lonely sun in winter.

He has no time to learn love's alphabet,
No time to wipe the murder from his eyes.

It is enough that he and she are met,
Alive. No rapture here, no strange surprise—
Only a fierce and brutal will to feel,
Kisses that bleed and lips as hard as steel.

J. S. MANIFOLD

Fife Tune

(For Sixth Platoon 308th I.T.C.)

One morning in spring
We marched from Devizes
All shapes and all sizes,
Like beads on a string,
But yet with a swing
We trod the bluemetal
And full of high fettle
We started to sing.

She ran down the stair
A twelve-year-old darling
And laughing and calling
She tossed her bright hair;
Then silent to stare
At the men flowing past her—
There were all she could master
Adoring her there.

It's seldom I'll see
A sweeter or prettier,
I doubt we'll forget her
In two years or three,

And lucky he'll be
She takes for a lover
While we are far over
The treacherous sea.

Suburban Lullaby

Fear the lights that cross the street,
Fear the blackout shadows grim,
Fear the bobby on his beat,
Fear the one that watches him:
  Fear the shock when they collide;
  Hurry, hurry home and hide.

Fear the lifting of the bolt;
Fear the fingers at the door:
Friendly hands may thumb a Colt,
Friendly things are friends no more.
  Voices crack that cry 'All's well'.
  Creep to bed and dream of hell.

History naked rides the sky;
Can you take him by the mane?
Is there time to justify?
Is there time to start again?
  Dare to hold or dare let go,
  What abysses gape below!

The Tomb of Lt John Learmonth, A.I.F.

'At the end on Crete he took to the hills, and said he'd fight it out with only a revolver. He was a great soldier . . .'

One of his men in a letter

This is not sorrow, this is work: I build
A cairn of words over a silent man,
My friend John Learmonth whom the Germans killed.

There was no word of hero in his plan;
Verse should have been his love and peace his trade,
But history turned him to a partisan.

Far from the battle as his bones are laid
Crete will remember him. Remember well,
Mountains of Crete, the Second Field Brigade!

Say Crete, and there is little more to tell
Of muddle tall as treachery, despair
And black defeat resounding like a bell;

But bring the magnifying focus near
And in contempt of muddle and defeat
The old heroic virtues still appear.

Australian blood where hot and icy meet
(James Hogg and Lermontov were of his kin)
Lie still and fertilize the fields of Crete.

*　　*　　*

Schoolboy, I watched his ballading begin:
Billy and bullocky and billabong,
Our properties of childhood, all were in.

I heard the air though not the undersong,
The fierceness and resolve; but all the same
They're the tradition, and tradition's strong.

Swagman and bushranger die hard, die game,
Die fighting, like that wild colonial boy—
Jack Dowling, says the ballad, was his name.

He also spun his pistol like a toy,
Turned to the hills like wolf or kangaroo,
And faced destruction with a bitter joy.

His freedom gave him nothing else to do
But set his back against his family tree
And fight the better for the fact he knew

He was as good as dead. Because the sea
Was closed and the air dark and the land lost,
'They'll never capture me alive', said he.

*   *   *

That's courage chemically pure, uncrossed
With sacrifice or duty or career,
Which counts and pays in ready coin the cost

Of holding course. Armies are not its sphere
Where all's contrived to achieve its counterfeit;
It swears with discipline, it's volunteer.

I could as hardly make a moral fit
Around it as around a lightning flash.
There is no moral, that's the point of it.

No moral. But I'm glad of this panache
That sparkles, as from flint, from us and steel,
True to no crown nor presidential sash

Nor flag nor fame. Let others mourn and feel
He died for nothing: nothings have their place.
While thus the kind and civilized conceal

This spring of unsuspected inward grace
And look on death as equals, I am filled
With queer affection for the human race.

JUDITH WRIGHT

The Company of Lovers

We meet and part now over all the world.
We, the lost company,
take hands together in the night, forget
the night in our brief happiness, silently.
We who sought many things, throw all away
for this one thing, one only,
remembering that in the narrow grave
we shall be lonely.

Death marshals up his armies round us now.
Their footsteps crowd too near.
Lock your warm hand above the chilling heart
and for a time I live without my fear.
Grope in the night to find me and embrace,
for the dark preludes of the drums begin,
and round us, round the company of lovers,
Death draws his cordons in.

Bullocky

Beside his heavy-shouldered team,
thirsty with drought and chilled with rain,
he weathered all the striding years
till they ran widdershins in his brain:

till the long solitary tracks,
etched deeper with each lurching load,
were populous before his eyes,
and fiends and angels used his road.

All the long straining journey grew
a mad apocalyptic dream,
and he old Moses, and the slaves
his suffering and stubborn team.

Then in his evening camp beneath
the half-light pillars of the trees,
he filled the steepled cone of night
with shouted prayers and prophecies,

while past the camp-fire's crimson ring
the star-struck darkness cupped him round,
and centuries of cattlebells
rang with their sweet uneasy sound.

Grass is across the waggon-tracks,
and plough strikes bone beneath the grass,
and vineyards cover all the slopes
where the dead teams were used to pass.

O vine, grow close upon that bone
and hold it with your rooted hand.
The prophet Moses feeds the grape,
and fruitful is the Promised Land.

Woman to Man

The eyeless labourer in the night,
the selfless, shapeless seed I hold,
builds for its resurrection-day—
silent and swift and deep from sight
foresees the unimagined light.

This is no child with a child's face;
this has no name to name it by:
yet you and I have known it well.
This is our hunter and our chase,
the third who lay in our embrace.

This is the strength that your arm knows,
the arc of flesh that is my breast,
the precise crystals of our eyes.
This is the blood's wild tree that grows
the intricate and folded rose.

This is the maker and the made;
this is the question and reply;
the blind head butting at the dark,
the blaze of light along the blade.
Oh hold me, for I am afraid.

Woman's Song

O move in me, my darling,
for now the sun must rise;
the sun that will draw open
the lids upon your eyes.

O wake in me, my darling.
The knife of day is bright
to cut the thread that binds you
within the flesh of night.

Today I lose and find you
whom yet my blood would keep—
would weave and sing around you
the spells and songs of sleep.

None but I shall know you
as none but I have known;
yet there's a death and a maiden
who wait for you alone;

so move in me, my darling,
whose debt I cannot pay.
Pain and the dark must claim you,
and passion and the day.

Legend

The blacksmith's boy went out with a rifle
and a black dog running behind.
Cobwebs snatched at his feet,
rivers hindered him,

thorn-branches caught at his eyes to make him blind
and the sky turned into an unlucky opal,
but he didn't mind.
I can break branches, I can swim rivers, I can stare out any
    spider I meet
said he to his dog and his rifle.

The blacksmith's boy went over the paddocks
with his old black hat on his head.
Mountains jumped in his way,
rocks rolled down on him,
and the old crow cried, You'll soon be dead!
And the rain came down like mattocks.
But he only said
I can climb mountains, I can dodge rocks, I can shoot an old
    crow any day,
and he went on over the paddocks.

When he came to the end of the day the sun began falling.
Up came the night ready to swallow him,
like the barrel of a gun,
like an old black hat,
like a black dog hungry to follow him.
Then the pigeon, the magpie and the dove began wailing
and the grass lay down to pillow him.
His rifle broke, his hat blew away and his dog was gone
and the sun was falling.

But in front of the night the rainbow stood on the mountain,
just as his heart foretold.
He ran like a hare,
he climbed like a fox,
he caught it in his hands, the colours and the cold—

like a bar of ice, like the column of a fountain,
like a ring of gold.
The pigeon, the magpie and the dove flew up to stare,
and the grass stood up again on the mountain.

The blacksmith's boy hung the rainbow on his shoulder
instead of his broken gun.
Lizards ran out to see,
snakes made way for him,
and the rainbow shone as brightly as the sun.
All the world said, Nobody is braver, nobody is bolder,
nobody else has done
anything to equal it. He went home as easy as could be,
with the swinging rainbow on his shoulder.

The Ancestors

That stream ran through the sunny grass so clear—
more polished than dew is, all one lilt of light.
We found our way up to the source, where stand
the fern-trees locked in endless age
under the smothering vine and the trees' night.

Their slow roots spread in mud and stone,
and in each notched trunk shaggy as an ape
crouches the ancestor, the dark bent foetus;
unopened eyes, face fixed in unexperienced sorrow,
and body contorted in the fern-tree's shape.

That sad, pre-history, unexpectant face—
I hear the answering sound of my blood, I know
these primitive fathers waiting for rebirth,

these children not yet born—the womb holds so
the moss-grown patience of the skull,
the old ape-knowledge of the embryo.

Their silent sleep is gathered round the spring
that feeds the living, thousand-lighted stream
up which we toiled into this timeless dream.

To a Child

When I was a child I saw
a burning bird in a tree.
I see became *I am*,
I am became *I see*.

In winter dawns of frost
the lamp swung in my hand.
The battered moon on the slope
lay like a dune of sand,

And in the trap at my feet
the rabbit leapt and prayed,
weeping blood, and crouched
when the light shone on the blade.

The sudden sun lit up
the webs from wire to wire;
the white webs, the white dew,
blazed with a holy fire.

Flame of light in the dew,
flame of blood on the bush
answered the whirling sun
and the voice of the early thrush.

I think of this for you.
I would not have you believe
the world is empty of truth
or that men must grieve,

but hear the song of the martyrs
out of a bush of fire—
'All is consumed with love;
all is renewed with desire.'

DAVID CAMPBELL

Soldier's Song

Though I march until I drop
And my bed is sand,
I have filled the desert's cup;
Harvested its land.
This is the song of the desert wind,
From the sphinx it blows:
The Murray's source is in the mind
And at a word it flows.

Though I climb the bitter rock,
Jungle for a bed,
I can muster such a flock
As never Falkiner bred.
This is the song of the tropic wind
Where the giant storm grows:
The Murray's source is in the mind
And at a word it flows.

DAVID CAMPBELL

Men in Green

Oh, there were fifteen men in green,
Each with a tommy-gun,
Who leapt into my plane at dawn;
We rose to meet the sun.

We set our course towards the east
And climbed into the day
Till the ribbed jungle underneath
Like a giant fossil lay.

We climbed towards the distant range
Where two white paws of cloud
Clutched at the shoulders of the pass;
The green men laughed aloud.

They did not fear the ape-like clouds
That climbed the mountain crest
And hung from twisted ropes of air
With thunder in their breast.

They did not fear the summer's sun,
In whose hot centre lie
A hundred hissing cannon shells
For the unwatchful eye.

And when on Dobadura's field
We landed, each man raised
His thumb towards the open sky;
But to their right I gazed.

For fifteen men in jungle green
Rose from the kunai grass
And came towards the plane. My men
In silence watched them pass;
It seemed they looked upon themselves
In Time's prophetic glass.

Oh, there were some leaned on a stick
And some on stretchers lay,
But few walked on their own two feet
In the early green of day.

They had not feared the ape-like cloud
That climbed the mountain crest;
They had not feared the summer's sun
With bullets for their breast.

Their eyes were bright, their looks were dull,
Their skin had turned to clay.
Nature had met them in the night
And stalked them in the day.

And I think still of men in green
On the Soputa track
With fifteen spitting tommy-guns
To keep a jungle back.

Night Sowing

O gentle, gentle land
Where the green ear shall grow,
Now you are edged with light:
The moon has crisped the fallow,
The furrows run with night.

This is the season's hour:
While couples are in bed,
I sow the paddocks late,
Scatter like sparks the seed
And see the dark ignite.

O gentle land, I sow
The heart's living grain.
Stars draw their harrows over,
Dews send their melting rain:
I meet you as a lover.

Heart of Light

Oh let the magpie blow
Full round days like drops of dew
That ring the earth and dome the sky
And tremble lest they spill
Drenching in cloud-burst sunshine our high hill.

In heart of dew we lie
Drowned in brief immortality
And watch our fair-haired children play
While the bird in the nest
Feels her eggs warm and aching at her breast.

Oh lock these days around
When to a gentle oneness bound
Hearts and little children play
And let such days atone
For those when we are many and alone.

The Monaro

Old Willie Gray will sit and stare
On one-tree-hill the whole day long
And green grass parrots fly in at his ear
And lay their eggs of rounded song
Leaving them there for the words to hatch
Like the floating seed from the thistle patch.

Old Willie Gray has a ten-mile stare
And his eyes are droving with a dream of sheep
Down raddled stock-routes to tread white air
Where old Willie Gray has a thought as deep
And as rounded as a river stone,
And over the paddocks goes the daylight moon.

Old Willie Gray has a lover's eye
And it goes over the twin bare hills
And the blond valleys to the bleached sky
Until it has come to a thought that fills
His mind with tenderness for this wild
Upland country and her suckling child.

Beach Queen

Saturday. Dove calls to running wave;
Light rocks in the hammocks of the swell
Dove-breasted. The city like a grave;
Flats without thoughts and clocks that doze—
Today, tomorrow, yesterday, forget,
In the dream of the humming-top, forget

Landladies with slippers off who knit
Today, tomorrow, out of yesterday.
For the dove cries to the running wave.
The city's elsewhere. Surely this is enough?
Blond multitudes upon the sand, a girl
Reading a book in sunglasses, the haze.
The acrobats and the ice-cream man,
The children building flats upon the sand.
The great ships drag horizons for her
And the tamed lions, the shouldering waves,
Slide to her sandalled feet and beach
The blond and casual to adore her.
Turn a page, how much more?
—In her garden Venus walks alone,
Turns and picks a fruit, aware, unknowing.
For oh, the sense sickens! The sun hurts,
Sand rasps and stings. What do the waves cry?
Last week they swept the beach and left it bare.
What do they say? In smoke on the blue air
An aircraft scribbles slogans on the sky.

VAL VALLIS

For This, the Tide

For this the tide flowed—
The fall of the flood,
Bleaching the bone of the shore;
Salt stinging the blood.

You are the shell it yields
To cup to my ears,
Distilling in desperate song
The surging years.

You sing how after the ebb
Rolls in the swell—
Rather the seas be lost
Than I lose the shell.

Too soon through the swollen tide
Leers the ribbed sand;
Enough that the touch of the shell
Be warm to my hand.

ROSEMARY DOBSON

The Missal

The lovely, lost, italic curve
Enrapt his soul. All day he stared
At A for Apple. Dimly heard
The beating of the holy wings
In D for Dove; but shut his ears
To sound's delight, instead preferred
The E of Eden, marked how stood
The mainstroke like a flaming sword.
Then F for Fall. How brief the flight
With dark descender, black as night!
The circumscribed, enchanting sweep
Of G was Goodness. Calm and strong
Gently it led his eye along
Delicious pastures of the page.
Then, overleaf, before him burned
The winged and serifed letter H
And Heaven was his to have and hold—
Oh missal wrought in holy gold.

The arrogance of earthly power—
Swash capitals for Kings and Men—
Diminished as he turned again
And summoned all his art to raise
The lettered record of his praise—
'Ere there was beast or fish or bird,
Before the Voice of Man was heard;
In the beginning was the Word'.

In my End is my Beginning

Draw a circle round me thrice
Arm's radius to this piece of earth;
Here's my Tom Tiddler's Land of danger,
Hazardous path to Death from Birth.

In this small orb is compassed wonder,
Passion, despair and state of grace.
I am that traveller who, returning,
Finds destination's starting-place.

For blood's my argument and reason,
And flesh is audible, and heart
Will know the way if these should fail,
And head will bear a steady part.

Wit's the one weapon for my fending,
Who travels farthest journeys light,
Save that the mind has faggots stored
To kindle fire on darkest night.

No fares for ferrying. If you will,
Saint Christopher, be with me still.

The Devil and the Angel (1)

Chancing upon the Devil in the doorway
(We being ourselves acquaintance of some standing),
The Prince of Darkness with his whips of flame
Slack and suspended idly from his arm,
Leaning against the lintel airily,
I tipped my halo in a friendly greeting.
'Sir,' I said, prudently polite, 'you know my friend
So honest, upright, jovial and kind?
Or is it, perhaps, that you mistake the entrance?'
He smiled and I fell silent while he knocked.
'When we go in,' he said, 'you think you'll see
A cornucopia of falling brilliance,
Light trembling from the chandelier and music,
Rustle of talk and laughter, flame on silk.
I think a shell, its hollows filled with shadows
Where spiders plot devices in the corners
And dust dries up the dregs from fallen glasses.'

We heard the footsteps, then the handle turning,
And, like the Queen of Spain and Queen of France,
We bowed each other entry through the doorway.

The Devil and the Angel (6)

The man was called Methuselah. I remember
I kept a memo folded in my garment;
Having a slight forgetfulness to combat
I arm myself against it.

Thus prepared
I journeyed to his dwelling; now through Heaven,
Cleaving the clouds with mission and importance,
And now on foot, joyful by turns or dreaming;
And dreaming thus I chanced upon the Devil.
'Friend,' I said (we observe these small refinements),
'Being met upon a singleness of purpose
We might perhaps continue on together.'
'Agreed,' he said; 'but look, the time is early,
The sun not far advanced beyond the valley;
I have two coins upon me and the path here
Is smooth enough—we'll toss a coin together.'
I argued back and forth and then remembered
As well to offer, to accept is courteous.
We tossed a round. The Devil won. Far off, Methuselah
Somewhat surprised, beyond his span of living,
Begat a son called Lamech. We tossed again,
I won. The chance was even. Meanwhile Methuselah
Turned two, three, then four hundred. Many sons
Rejoiced his age. 'Time goes', I cried. The Devil
In silence tossed again. Methuselah
Begat near twenty daughters. 'Time', I said to the Devil;
'Time, PLEASE', I said. He pocketed the pennies.

Methuselah turned to greet us from his deathbed.
And round him half a hundred sons and daughters
Mourned and lamented his departing spirit.

NAN McDONALD

Wet Summer : Botanic Gardens

Under the low dark sky and the sodden leaves
Poor Summer bared her shoulder with coy grace,
Her marble flesh streaked with mortality.
Her sheaf of wheat lay mildewed on her arm,
Her eyes stared vacant from her tear-stained face
On paths empty at noon, on glooms beneath
Great fig-trees, where the drop of rotting fruit
Broke the warm, damp hush, on unbelievable green
Of wet grass still unfaded by the sun
In this strange season. Once we laughed to see
That foolish white thing named for the brazen queen
Whose sword we knew, the fierce and splendid one.

But tonight, alone with the steady sound of rain,
I do not smile, seeing her image there
On the haunted edge of sleep—the blackening marble,
The blind and weeping eyes, the ruined grain—
Seeing this season of the world's despair.

NANCY KEESING

Old Men

Today I have been thinking of very old men,
So old that death, standing just at their backs,
Wears no disguise for them but is exactly
As each of them has come to think death looks.
I have been thinking of withered static bodies.
Tattered end-papers guarding wonderful books.

And it has appeared to me also that they resemble
Cities shrouded by a grey, sweeping rain;
They are simplified, they are like shapes reduced to angles.
The lowest common denominator of all they are and have
    been.
Dim trees in the park had that aspect this morning,
Even their colours reduced, greyed down, not green;

Trees merely forms, as much of the city as mortar,
Bound to the streets or the spires by the sheets of rain,
Or like old men with a common cover of years,
Removing their age from their youth, making them wise
Or lending illusion of knowledge, making them seem
Marvellously sage. Old men blink tired eyes,

Move cracking lips with effort and hesitation
Muttering softly (dead leaves wash to the grass).
They discourse, not of today but of other time,
While constantly that shadow which unnoticed stole
Behind each man, his final simplicity,
Waits the last wisdom, the merging of past with whole.

DAVID ROWBOTHAM

Little White Fox

Little white fox, I love you,
    And when with limb to limb
We lie while waits the Hunter
    I love your body slim.

Think not that the clover withers,
    That thrushes sing to fall,
But let your lips of springtime
    Devour and close on all.

They who mate in willows,
    Those who dream by the sea,
Make this sweet intermission
    Their mind and memory.

Little white fox, I love you,
    And when with limb to limb
We lie while halts the Hunter
    I am grateful to him.

The Moment

It is the reaching out into the dark
Where Youth's planetary flame revolves in a flow
Of light and days. It is the looking up
When even the most familiar sounds break
And the looking down when smallest voices speak.
It is man listening like a tree and loving
With an open-hearted love. It is the growing
Toward that mature moment of joy when all
That pleases may become an elixir
Of some forgotten wonder, now remembered.
And the wonder is ours and the quality of Always.
It is the rose out of the snow and the bird
Out of the bough
When the world is known not to be green forever.

JOHN HENDERSON

Of Love and Time

'Run faster, love,' you say and I
Grow dizzy asking why and why.
'Run faster, love, the rival night
Runs down our avenue of light;
Run faster, love, my Image shines
Upon the stations of the signs.'

Sharpen the blade I must, and tear
This Moon away, these Stars, this hair
Whose weeping gold blinds me until
The dazzle in my eyes is still.
'Run faster, love!' But who could cut
A pathway where her eyelids shut
Her dreaming in a sphere of blue
I dare not let my thought walk through?

MARY FINNIN

Sarah Lorton

Was hunting bigger prey and came upon her—
Sarah Lorton, with her death about her.

Through another old year seeking another—
Hugh Niven, the young overlander from Sydney,
(Son of Daniel Niven, merchant, Glasgow),
Killed by his horse at Sutherland's Creek in 'thirty-nine.

It was to fill out this man's obsequies and round his story,
That I searched in the stone keep where cobwebs tether book
    to book
In a grey chain of time for the recorder.

Calm on the yellowing page was Sarah's name,
How, her poor shift for shroud,
She was buried to the kind words of Andrew Love—
(First pastor here, and she his pastoral grieve)—
Sarah Lorton, with her death upon her.

'By drowning, a poor female, aged forty.'
But she was younger—thirty-three—
When she slipped from the bank below the immigrant
    barracks,
With a pitcher to fill at Barwon Breakwater,
That hot Thursday in December eighteen-forty.

But no Ophelia in long purples palled,
With noble youth to garland her still beauty,
She floated down the stream remembering
The tears of little things that make us glad—
The lacquer on a cat-faced button box,
Red velvet curtains, yellow kitchen clocks—
While black swans, plumed and stately on the green,
Were Caroline Newcomb, Charlotte Fisher, riding
Down the flanks of Strawberry Hill to dole out tracts
To the brickmakers, blue in their stubborn marsh clay.
('To make them good, and keep the drink away.'
O sidelong gait that after grog shop shuts,
Stumps slugfoot home to iceberg eyes and hearts!)
The stench of mutton-fat, the barracks fires,
Sealed off the river mist on Sarah's day.

Though voice to voice rings down the hollow years
Always death leaps the threshold where our ears
Take over from the past.
Almost I hear them now:—
David Fisher, testy when old because no one
Could well remember all that he had seen;
Andrew Love, whose voice was all affection,
Most dear in consolation;
And Fyans, with the bite of Ulster mulled
By twenty years of warm colonial days.

This side of life she had no time to spare;
But there—
Where Sarah's gone—
No conscience tolls a passing-bell for pleasure.
They pluck blanched flowers in the valley of the moon,
Sarah Lorton and her death together.

Three Trees at Solstice

Comes with autumn the spent moment,
When, polarized to stillness,
The soul thereafter waits on death
As oaks on winter,
As oaks by winter water.
So stands the sun for springing and failing time;
And a life ending is less than a stream failing
Until, sunk deep in a white meander—
Black clouds come down like swans at brood,
And flows again the white water.

The silver tree of the stream
Fails not for the sea,
Nor for thirst-hewn rocks of the valley;
But fails the red, bright tree
In each man's breast—
Drooping to winter's rest;
Fails the yellow tree
Of each day's light—
Fails from sight,
Fails in the west.

MAX HARRIS

Lullaby

Girl with eyes like dying flowers,
come near and close them and shut out
the elegant spring. You have lived hours
on the moon's lips among night flowers.

If your hand is cold and wet
and your thoughts a cruel cage
let your body stretch to me and set
its marble like disaster in my flesh.

Now your golden hair lies dead
and your arms, so white and brown.
The thorn and the storm your eyes have shed
and they are in me and you are dead.

The Plowman

My sad great Piers that met a small field flower,
how well that bole your brain becomes the lilted thought
that curved in mystic flight above the seven sins
leaving your coarse hands helpless, singing at a plow.

My sad great Piers that met a small field flower,
such petals closed about the dark vernacular of your sex
you stammered as trapped, were hunted like a rose,
leaving your coarse hands helpless, singing at a plow.

My sad great Piers that met a small field flower,
and now small torment, the wind-swung angel's enigma,
a breath of quaint ecstasy in parabolas of quiet
and your coarse hands helpless, singing at a plow.

Martin Buber in the Pub

My friends are borne to one another
By their lack of something to say;
The weight of inward thought is lifted
And they float to each other
Like paper darts: they offer the salt of themselves
Arab-like in hotels,
Humbler than they would have you believe.
Humanity is the smallest coin for tipping.
Allen relates a host of grandiose lies . . .
These are the wafers of our religion.

Barnes is the butt of malice,
An unmysterious drinking of the blood . . .
And the seas may boil outside. No doubt they do.
But we are in a silence of some sort,
Exchanging shells, which placed against the ear,
Occasionally echo the throbbing of a heart.

GEOFFREY DUTTON

Nightflight and Sunrise

The flux of night is power and will, slid
Like a coined sun into the dark horizon.
Shadows hollow out the convex earth
Of mystery, till the hills
Of the knuckles are one with the mountains of the moon.

'Who can distinguish darkness from the soul?'
The explorer lightless beyond the wings, by red
And green exalted and tore out the eyes
Of cat and fox. The body
Was entered, as will is seldom, by the soul.

Riding the groundswell of the dark is the impulse
Born of love, whose only maps of light
Are a green beam, wind in a flame's motion
Of flares that sit like jewels
While bushfires on a fox's brush race hills
And hounds in air. Through their consuming blows
The wind of planets, cut keener past the cheek
Than knives of light along the unseen roads.
The face by the fire, shadowed like a pirate,
Holds life in eyes that judge,
Eased back and ruddered to the fatal ground.

But the armoured sun infiltrates the vast dark miles,
Will and its body spring forward like shadows,
And the airman sees behind the secret hedge
The movements of the morning.
The flux of night becomes the will to live

Behind a death whirled more sudden than scythe
In mist of a propellor, fledged gently
In the veiled hills and creeks veined like a walnut.
The flame in the black well
Is gone. But the airman's hand stroked skin

Of the cosmic heart and counted the beats from day.
He airborne and alone was stressed of stars
And entered the source of all activity.
As shadows leap away
From light, so with their substance he awaits the night.

A Prisoner Freed

The wind slammed shut the door and he remembered
The last bolt home, final clang of despair,
Saw stone rise through the carpet and the moon
Lie barred across the floor. Suddenly he knew,
Only memory can lay bare actuality
And he who shuts his eyes alone can see.

Through the dissolving walls he felt the night
Fall from him, come down five sides of air
And lock him in ennui, softly as a fog,
With death for lover in his waiting bed.
The vacant moving light is a clock of comfort
And points the hunger in satiety

That sees him shuffle uneasily into the future
Like a drunkard into a church.   The actual hour
Of love alone is apprehended
As a triumph and a death, the sour remainder
Is the day of bone and blood trying to fight
With hand and eye the unseen enemy of the mind.

Now a kindly jailer turns him
On a key of days, a padlock on the mind
That lies most heavy as intangible,
Smiling that his is the subtlest captivity being free,
Linked on an unseen leash like gravity
To earth, and death still virgin on the sheet.

PATRICIA EXCELL

Forgotten Objects on a Beach

Sea-smooth stones imprison a moon
On the shore where the winds hide
In purple shells, delicate and known from childhood.

I am a sea-wanderer through dreams—
Retracing calligraphy of wave and sand,
Touching again weed and driftwood;

Strange shapes that are half memories—
Laughter and sand-dune-silence! The child's
White joy at the merging of two worlds.

I plunge my hands into this shining space,
Hold sea-sculpture and the moon
On the shadowless beach.

I re-enter a familiar world. But now
The once heard sound I know to be
Chirico's horses trampling on the shore.

FRANCIS WEBB

For My Grandfather

When the ropes droop and loosen, and the gust
Piecemeal upon a widening quietness fails,
Fail breath and spirit; against the bony mast
Work in like skin the frayed and slackened sails.
In the green lull where ribs and keel lie wrecked,
Wrapped in the sodden, enigmatic sand,
Things that ache sunward, seaward, with him locked,
Tug at the rigging of the dead ship-lover's hand.
Though no wind's whitening eloquence may fill
Drowned canvas with the steady bulge of breath,
Doubling for past, for future, are never still
The bones ambiguous with life and death.

Dusk over Bradley's Head: a feeble gull
Whose sinking body is the past at edge
Of form and nothing: here the beautiful
Letona gybes, off the spray-shaken ledge.
And to those years, dusk comes but as a rift
In the flesh of sunlight, closed by memory:
Shells stir in the pull of water, lift
Fragile and holy faces to the sky.
My years and yours are scrawled upon this air
Rapped by the gavel of my living breath:
Rather than time upon my wrist I wear
The dial, the four quarters of your death.

The Gunner

When the gunner spoke in his sleep the hut was still,
Uneasily strapped to the reckless wheel of his will;
Silence, humble, directionless as fog,
Lifted, and minutes were rhythmical on the log;

While slipstream plucked at a wafer of glass and steel,
Engines sliced and scooped at the air's thin wall,
And those dim spars dislodged from the moon became
Red thongs of tracer whipping boards aflame.

Listening, you crouched in the turret, watchful and taut
—*Bogey two thousand, skipper, corkscrew to port*—
Marvellous, the voice: driving electric fires
Through the panel of sleep, the black plugs, trailing wires.

The world spoke through its dream, being deaf and blind,
Its words were those of the dream, yet you might find
Forgotten genius, control, alive in this deep
Instinctive resistance to the perils of sleep.

Laid Off

I. *The Bureau, and Later*

Outside the Bureau all the trams and trains
Prattled securely, with us out of air
To ply like bits of refuse among drains
Nudging each other nastily when it rains.

Only the suck or slap of rubber sole
At marble was our case and hearing. Spare
Butts, down to earth, drafted one smoky scroll
For factory, office, wharf, and police patrol.

I pitied the man behind the counter, who'd
Hear us be cruelly serious, hear us swear,
Be funny, No-speak-English—see us bowed
Under the weight of tools to make him God.

Later:—this swine with platitudinous
Squeaks of his oily leather-bottomed chair
Makes up his mouth to tell me less and less
And plays at being Satan, with more success.

To the most dangerous driver, righteous heat,
Our traffic-lights are neither here nor there.
I stare at the pock-marked baby while I eat
And walk past the blind mouth-organist on the street.

II. *Hard-luck Story*

'Yes, this is the stop for Central. Yes, right here.
Cold weather? Right, I'll try a tailor-made'—
Breaking the ice is moving mountains, sheer
Bravado if there's no time for a prayer.

Frayed eyelids button on to me; this thin
Lip of the cold snap will not have me wade
Or even pet my carefully nourished skin
To reassure it before plunging in.

Taxes and breadless children swim or drown
Without mercy inside his overcoat. Afraid?
So I am—but citizens pay to see again
A great dramatist's aquarium of pain.

His bony, dickering, artist's hands attach
Years to my ears; from their ice-box of shade
Castles crane forward, puff themselves up, and watch
For the foolhardy twinkle of my match.

Morgan's Country

This is Morgan's country: now steady, Bill
(Stunted and grey, hunted and murderous).
Squeeze for the first pressure. Shoot to kill.

Five: a star dozing in its cold cavern.
Six: first shuffle of boards in the cold house.
And the sun lagging on seven.

The grey wolf at his breakfast. He cannot think
Why he must make haste, unless because their eyes
Are poison at every well where he might drink.

Unless because their gabbling voices force
The doors of his grandeur, first terror, then only hate.
Now terror again. Dust swarms under the doors.

Ashes drift on the dead-sea shadow of his plate.
Why should he heed them? What to do but kill
When his angel howls, when the sounds reverberate

In the last grey pipe of his brain? At the window sill
A blowfly strums on two strings of air:
Ambush and slaughter tingling against the lull.

But the Cave, his mother, is close beside his chair,
Her sunless face scribbled with cobwebs, bones
Rattling in her throat as she speaks. And there

The stone Look-out, his towering father, leans
Like a splinter from the seamed palm of the plain.
Their counsel of thunder arms him. A threat of rain.

Seven: and a blaze fiercer than the sun.
The wind struggles in the arms of the starved tree:
The temple breaks on a threadbare mat of grass.

Eight: even under the sun's trajectory
This country looks grey, hunted and murderous.

From *A View of Montreal*

I. *Cartier at St Malo*

At a certain time in life it becomes essential
To worry about St Malo. Novelty is dangerous:
The white antlers of the floe; Belle Isle in ruins—
Collisions of stone and spray—yet abiding, the pillar
And surly station of disorder.
If hollow-cheeked Anticosti
Should come too often, like a waterfall in sleep,
Opening and closing his senseless eyes, wagging his silver
Dankness of hair (this prophet convulsed) and whistling
Directions to the wind through his wicked shining teeth:
Well, we might come to take him for a roadstead light.
Moreover there is little genuine merit in dying
Of scurvy among barbarians. Suppose that a fisherman
Falls to his death in our natural, antique waters:
What consolations, what golden devices of usage
As he cries at the masthead, wandering footloose, a moment

Abandons himself to the vague forests of air,
Strikes cleanly, and is not wasted! (Indeed, with the feeding
Habits of fish . . . but this is the jest of a veteran.)
He is not of our knowledge, true. He is dead, he is spent,
But an image flowers on this sky and this casual water,
These arbours of order. Our unease, but our exaltation;
Of winter, and radiant; of death, and the marriage-bed.
A girl weeps—but candles enfeature the faces
Of the Saints, but the old bells
Assault and transfigure our whole rich foreshores of silence.

It is to this we have come as the husbandman
Retired with his new, strange bounty of contemplation:
To the mild ways of the coastal sun, to the waves
Docile yet proud as sheaves, tossing their heavy
Glittering heads, and winnowed upon the Sillon.
This never-to-be-spoiled acreage! Others will store
Against our winters its grey bundles of faggots—
The mackerel, John Dory in his crushed mail—
When ships are byred on the slipway.
          And whence are we come?
Strictly speaking, from nowhere. Here is St Malo:
Will you once breathe St Malo
And say there is another air? or say (as a man of discernment)
That childhood is *there*, age *there*, and between is anything?

Confronting the brawny angel of the storm, contending
With the hideous moccasined runner, perhaps I strove
Only for this: that sleep become a haspless door,
As now—a wakefulness. Catherine beside me is quiet;
In this temperate swaying of time, cajolement of passion,
We do not strain to each other:
I am not sailing away tomorrow morning.

But these, the newcomers, up at the crack of dawn,
Their faces as the first light vital, various as towns,
Serene in a stance, or perishing nobly
On the world's most foreign, most slippery ledge (while always
The Court and their sweethearts are somehow close by to
    observe them)—
These I must teach. I say to them, they were better
To lay all petitions on the sure prayer-wheel of the compass
Rather than on the omen or the intention,
As for instance St Elmo's eaglet of fire in the shrouds
Or a sleeping sailor's revelation of landfall.
But remains the white tower of our Service
Whereto all words must aspire; therefore, in concluding,
I counsel them not to belittle the good intention:
For while thirst is a rasp whetted on the bitter
Coarse salt of the sea, while the shark's tooth is a ribbon
Of candid and vicious fire, while hunger and disease
Are, when we come to them, pain and there is nothing
Nothing but pain, neither truth nor good nor evil
In fifty worlds—still beyond these worlds is another.
Let a ship be taken by the ice, squeezed in the scrawny
Fingers of the frozen element, clasped, and racked, and
    splintered,
Driven like a living nail into the heaving bloodless
Face of the cold and clenched there: yet will come back
A Word or a Name.
        If merely a piece of wreckage,
Troubling, shifting in its marble, working like a statue
But cause of its own creation:
Tilting and turning downward among the vigilant
Tapering eyes of the dead, past the locked wheel
And lashings derisive of north and south: thence upward.
In the sun's circles and torrents a seabird

Rapt and lighted and moving,
In the storm marred and perplexed, unresting at the seven
Beaches of sin, nor turning back at the blasphemous
Mirage, the Gates of Herakles swinging outward,
It will come home to us. The more to be marvelled at
For its drapings of terror.
          It is with these words
I cancel myself: irony were a sacrilege,
It is here they take fire, speak loudly, brush me aside,
They burn, their wild humours
Come to the boil in them: they *must* see the King!

In the gale of illusion will march the honest tree,
Self-flagellant, murmuring
Against its gift, the knowing, the queer science—
Mortality, an ague rocking to the root.
On the morrow, mortality is strength. I have known them
    stir me:
St Malo a falsehood; nothing truthful but the green
Loitering disconsolate wind-crossed figure of the sea
In an old archway; nothing to seek but the Saguenay,
Myth of jewels and miles, fact of murder and deceit;
Nothing enduring but Hochelaga, the village
Where our language was wrenched by the red screeching
    birds.
Then, rubbing at starlight, the mast of an anchored ship
Twitches—these tiny movements of peace; then dawn,
Lover, discoverer, charts our St Malo with wakening
Legends and lights; and return is out of the question.

VINCENT BUCKLEY

Korea

Our tree breaks in this earth, a fallow life
Consenting to its rape, where soldiers trudge
The sunken roads, and blackness invades the air
Till the vast world is centred on this grief.

For the roads join in fear; and one man's pain
Is each man's living scar. The anguish burns
Through commentaries, assortments, résumés,
Spoken between another's death and mine.

A night of armies, magnified till they seem
The settled world converging on its death
And less than honour, gathers all our years
In the wind-driven savage waters of a dream;

And more than this: A land that had seemed human
Is marked and measured now in squares of power,
And all her burning veins, proud flesh erased
(The cry of her priests, the soft speech of her women)

In a cry that gives the world an emphasis
Greater than body's weight, or the dumb sea's
Exact and heavy measuring of her shores.
Cry, wounded land! Pity has words for this

Affronted wisdom of the race, for the blood
In shivering tides, rocking its shallow bed
To a tumult greater than birth, or borne
Onward in darkened and accosting flood.

Yet who of us all, gods with alien faces,
Will come in this night to drain their brimming cup,
Free among the dead, in a dead city,
Where only anger and fear have left their traces?

Who will go guarantor for love, or make
Their anguish payment of the world's debt
And sad arrears of sin? I only know them
As human vessels that a cry will break.

A white-grained stone, a cypress, and a wall
On pious guard are our tribute to the dead
Whom pity has smoothed back with tireless hands;
And how much more a city's burial

That died in the plague of war. For here at least
Is memory, at least hands to smooth
The eyes, and chamber limbs—but none will tend
This tree of anger planted in the East

To cast its blossoms over all the world,
And leaves of men, (the tumult of the bones),
Turned round and round in the unceasing fire
Where at the heart a serpent lies uncurled.

And eyes, must eyes consent, as murders leash
The stretch and nervous temper of the earth,
To glimpse the dewy fallen universe
And Eve with cities tumbling from her flesh?

CHARLES OSBORNE

So Fly by Night

So fly by night,
my phrase will not pursue you
through darkness and the
evil that men do.
Your flirting breath may dance
on time and passion,
or hide from sorrow
in a word or two.

Yet be not sad,
for gentleness surrounds you,
and though I move without
your gay deceit,
I know that you with time
and love will find me,
and bless, promiscuous truth,
the day we meet.

JOHN PHILIP

The Subject of the Bishop's Miracle

I

First get out the map and look at the country.

Here the retractive turtles frustrate the foolish dogs
and the hot sun shines through the amber
translucent goannas that climb the brigalow

233

and the ironbark. Here the shower of crested
pigeons is shaken from the tumescent bottle-trees
and the butcher-bird turns the burden of the cedars
to a golden swarm of bells.

And here the swaying uncorseted emus gallop past
the prickly pear, and the prickly pear is a bright green
balancing feat of flabby paws
displaying their sure geometry of spines
and the small magenta pear;
and the innocent gecko causes argument
about his power of colour change.

And here the huge red peering cattle and the sunflowers
make a brittle wilderness of eyes; and the ibis
and the plump cormorant perch in the grey plumbing
of the crooked pandanus that reaches out
toward the steep green islands
and the clear deep pools, kaleidoscopes
for boughs of coral and the aniline fish.

II

Now observe the inset in the corner.

This is the city of toy trains and the library full of tomcats,
and the big bright petals falling from the trees
into the eyes of the people are lottery tickets.
This is the city. Do you hear the weeping figs and the arrogant
cockroaches
and the churchbells thudding pegleg down the long streets?
This is the city. Can you taste the hardness of the water
and the yellow goodness of the beer? This is the prison and the
carnival.

The city has its river. True, there are sewage outfalls,
but also bridges and barges and the pieces of green bank.
And here by the river is a high room,
finite, without spiders.

III

There is no brandy left in the high room,
but she is there, she whom I love and hate.
This is she, the dreamer of the double dream,
the subject of the bishop's miracle.
Do you observe her eyes
and the broken land behind?

IV

Can you see the birdless country of those eyes?
The forest of young hands patiently hammering nails
with sickles; the acres of young arms
slowly reaping the harvest with claw hammers.
But see, on the cloud-bruised hill,
the gentle pageant of nuns, like thin black cows,
wear a sure path to water and the city built
of books and bells and broken banners.

V

But yet, within the city, who is the
Mother Superior and who the madam of the house?
Are the girls engaged in douches or in decades?
And on the stained window, Mary
And the Black Madonna tear each other's hair;
Theresa tosses, and the disappointed
gardeners push the smashed earth back
to the dark unpeopled grave.

VI

Though the unicorn mourns, entangled in the rose-tree,
though the lion roars in the whitewashed cage of crosses,
Demeter gives her breasts to the sure day
and opens her flanks to the pain and the joy
and the making of skulls. Demeter dances
in the stony clearing, with bleeding feet
and the deep song warming her lips.

HAL PORTER

Bi-focal

The Hills are verdigris and sallow;
the Slopes are tattooed jade and fallow;
mackerel Cloud and woaded Sky
over the leopard Acres lie.

My Heart is magpie, mottled, marbled;
This in my Heart with That is garbled;
my Memories and Dreams I note
are harlequin as Joseph's Coat.

Freckled with Heaven, flecked with Hell,
yet is this World of Tortoiseshell
not, with its Colours tessellated,
to my motley Soul related:

Zebra with Anguish, Tiger with Yearnings,
a Pepper-and-Salt of Ice and Burnings,
I find in Mosaic no Relief:
Striae of Grief by Grief by Grief.

BARRIE REID

St Kilda

The nights are warm again
the crowds go wandering
and loiter by the wall
   as if occasionally
breezes might walk on the sea
    lying half enclosed
    half an eye wearily
and no occasion at all.

In the park that goes
by the Royal Yacht Club
lovers lie like the news
   that no breeze blows.
Some strangely come to love
two minutes from the tram.
    Others halfhearted come
    to nothing worth speaking of.

At midnight that bright star
goes out at the end of the street
    and occasionally uneasily
    halfheartedly to and fro
the wandering voices meet
nothing worth speaking to:
I'm a woman with a husband!
    Good luck to you.

Nothing

I

Your eyes open;
no light nor dark of love
open, eyes are eyes no more,
and neither words nor echo stir,
no embrace, no question to the storm
of the world, no answer.
Nothing is your one familiar.
The day fades from the day's relentless calm.
What then? So fallen out of love,
falling, falling, through the unknowing air,
what carries you? what begins
your very breathing, your absence
from the scream you cannot form,
and the half-dreamt, half-sought idea
of making a move, going out of the room,
go where? running to your self
or someone, with what self?
can find no home
even in the heartbeat of terror
the similitude of silence. Nothing
says all, and those who have come
from the desert say, This is too far.
There is Nothing here.

II

Be still. Be still for here
is what cannot be known
to the heart's words, in that centre
over what cannot be called in time

somewhere is visible
and will hold you, the native
world, eternally turning towards you
what is most natural—
even now towards you
where nothing becomes you
and you become nothing at all.
Arise like morning held in clarity
memory of this deepest
aquamarine, walk
either in peace or terror
lightly over the water, there
over the airy tents of the water
while you go quietly
where the light breaks
and is submarine, under the water
among these early things, turning time
anew to such a treasure and
returning originally to this silence
where each is alone and for this time
our peace and terror break along the shore.

III

Yet trees cannot describe
roses cannot fail
the beasts have voices that are not beast voices;
at times we cannot speak—
that is our cannot speaking.
All our words say us,
the noises of our human being,
explicit heart, translucent mind,
to heart and mind obscure
describing, failing.

The first thing said is said, is everything,
says everything, says nothing,
is beginning—hear the echoes
returning, confusing
the thing that was said (search for it,
say it again). Yet
the tree falls, uprooted, torn out,
we cannot place the word to save its life;
anguish is our word and says us only—
and this snow-kitten's death
says our pain; we cannot say
their pain, or call it humble,
or silence even, their lives are about us
and all we say says us—
uprooted, the clearest image
of that great tree torn,
what does it say? silence
surrounds my heart, my silence
to my silence, in the night,
that clearest image taken,
my word to my word,
caught in the beginning,
in the ending,
in my human being.

IV

Those who live alone in rooms
are perhaps lucky in this
that there as they open the door
in or out to loneliness
there is no lover or child to run
forward quickly, enclosing them with otherness.

Here sometimes they pause upon clarity:
I am here and to this I am this.

Such is their nakedness.
You would say: Their love
has come to nothing after all,
there is no other here, or anywhere—
nothing to take the strain, nothing
between each man. Here
in distance, in exile, above
all, shall love grow—
this is its very air.

For there is nothing here
there are no names for you to go by now
there is no prayer
only a heart beating, below
all, and being human
is free to move
into that nothing which is love.

V

Then hold the mirror to this falling star
oracular, dispassionate, remote,
and hold it at a distance and come near
and is it falling? Are you falling?

The paper ribbon to the paper boat
holds, holds hard out on this ocean of the air
but do not cling to it, things have no weight
and will hold. Is that star falling,

or echoing, is that voice crying falling
or are you somewhere out of sound
out of harbour? O turn the world around,
it is the lightening, fading star of morning.

RAY MATHEW

Young Man's Fancy

Come tomorrow night,
or don't come ever.
The moon will give light
enough for a lover.

I'll stand in the deep dark
of a gum-tree's shadow,
but you'll find me all right
if you really want to.

But I won't wait long,
You must come if you're coming.
Without talk of wrong
or breakfast at morning.

If they find out
just say you were walking
to see if the night
could stop a head aching.

And don't mention me
because I don't own you.
We just happen to meet;
I don't really know you.

Yes, I want you to come,
with the moon in your hair.
And the moon in your eyes
as you look for me there.

Yes, I want you to come,
but I'll promise you nothing.
And if you're not game
then I still won't be crying.

But come tomorrow night
or don't come ever.
I won't spend two nights
waiting for a lover.

Let us not Pretend

Let us not pretend this is a war of adults.
Let us confess it is a war of children,
Little children—pushing soldiers from a table.
Only children could not realise the stopping of a sense
The sudden ceasing of delight,
Only children could pick them up again
And set them right.

You take this and I'll bomb yours.
Why do you knock them down?—Because.
I own the table; you have the floor.
Isn't it great fun having a war?

Let us not pretend this is a war of adults;
It is a war of ordinary children—
Children with running noses and much noise.

It is their great eyes that lie so still,
And their white bones
That crumble huge and silent
Among the golden stones.

Let us not rejoice in the returning soldiers;
They have been too much outside humanity.
And not cry out for their wasted lives;
Adult lives are never wholly wasted.
Only the children have need of our thinking . . .
So thoughtlessly they sinned,
The callous children who caused it all—
Their flesh paler than the summer wind.

In the city of great flies,
It is their teeth that are scattered, their flesh that is stinking
To the crow's eyes.

Picnic

The sudden sun, and the white spring rain
Is bright on the ground as cold white wine.
Give me a bluebell-cup, my love,
For we shall never come again
To this clean, and young, Australian time.

Last night we drank our wealth in wine
As red as our blood, as cheap as rain.
Give me your lips to drink, my love,
For we have very little time,
We shall not find this place again.

I drink a toast to this clean, white rain
That lightens in the heart like wine.
Give me your hand to hold my love,
For I will never come again
With you, with love, to such a time.

The Poems come Easier

The poems come easier
when you're very tired
with your head on the pillow
so the thoughts can creep.
But the head is heavier,
the pencil bigger,
and the words fall asleep.

The poems come easier
when the heart's a black crow
and your eyes scoop hollows
in the hard earth's glare.
But the thought is self-pity,
the tune monotonous,
and your note-book's not there.

The poems come easier
when your body shouts singing
because you're beside her
though you're miles apart.
But the song is a wild duck
not easy catching,
and it flies to the calm
in the heart of your heart.

But the poems come easiest
when you're really belonging,
and the deep earth and the dark sea
find in you home.
Then the bees that were buzzing
like flies at your eyelids
bring yellow-sun pollen
with song to the comb.

SOURCES OF THE POEMS

Charles Harpur:
'A Midsummer Noon in the Australian Forest' from *Poems*, George Robertson, 1883.

Daniel Deniehy:
'To His Wife' from *An Australasian Anthology*, Collins, 1946.

Henry Kendall:
'Prefatory Sonnet' from *Leaves from Australian Forests*, George Robertson, 1869.

William Gay:
'The Crazy World' from *The Poetical Works of William Gay*, Lothian, 1911.

Barcroft Henry Boake:
'Where the Dead Men Lie' from *Where the Dead Men Lie*, Angus & Robertson, 1913.

Bernard O'Dowd:
'Love and Sacrifice' from *Collected Poems of Bernard O'Dowd*, Lothian, 1941.

Henry Lawson:
'The Roaring Days' from *The Poetical Works of Henry Lawson*, Angus & Robertson, 1944.

Christopher Brennan:
'We Woke Together' from *XXI Poems*, Angus & Robertson, 1897.
'Let us Go Down' from *Poems*, G. B. Philp & Son, 1913.
'Sweet Silence after Bells' from *Poems*, G. B. Philp & Son, 1913
'My Heart was Wandering' from *Poems*, G. B. Philp & Son, 1913.
'The Years that Go to Make Me Man' from *Poems*, G. B. Philp & Son, 1913.
'What Do I Know?' from *Poems*, G. B. Philp & Son, 1913.
'How Old is My Heart?' from *Poems*, G. B. Philp & Son, 1913.
'O Desolate Eves' from *Poems*, G. B. Philp & Son, 1913.
'I Said, This Misery Must End' from *Poems*, G. B. Philp & Son, 1913.

John Shaw Neilson:

'Song be Delicate' from *Collected Poems*, Lothian, 1934.
'To a Blue Flower' from *Collected Poems*, Lothian, 1934.
'Break of Day' from *Collected Poems*, Lothian, 1934.
''Tis the White Plum Tree' from *Collected Poems*, Lothian, 1934.
'The Orange Tree' from *Collected Poems*, Lothian, 1934.
'Stony Town' from *Collected Poems*, Lothian, 1934.
'Schoolgirls Hastening' from *Collected Poems*, Lothian, 1934.
'I Spoke to the Violet' from *Beauty Imposes*, Angus & Robertson, 1938.

William Dyson:

'Death is but Death' from *Poems in Memory of a Wife*, Cecil Palmer, 1919.

Leon Gellert:

'Before Action' from *Songs of a Campaign*, G. Hassell & Co., 1917.
'In the Trench' from *Songs of a Campaign*, G. Hassell & Co., 1917.
'These Men' from *Songs of a Campaign*, G. Hassell & Co., 1917.

Furnley Maurice:

'To God: From the Warring Nations' (selections) from *Poems*, Lothian, 1944.
'The Gully' (selections) from *Poems*, Lothian, 1944.
'The Victoria Markets Recollected in Tranquillity' from *Poems*, Lothian, 1944.

William Baylebridge:

'Wherever I Go' from *Selected Poems*, Gordon & Gotch, 1919.
'Who questions if the punctual sun unbars' from *Love Redeemed*, Tallabila Press, 1939.
'When tongues will tax me in the public ear' from *A Wreath*, privately printed, c.1939.
'The utile canons, the set codes of priests' from *Love Redeemed*, Tallabila Press, 1939.
'The Ampler Circumscription' from *This Vital Flesh*, Tallabila Press, 1939.
'The brain, the blood, the busy thews' from *This Vital Flesh*, Tallabila Press, 1939.
'I worshipped, when my veins were fresh' from *This Vital Flesh*, Tallabila Press, 1939.
'All that I am to Earth belongs' from *This Vital Flesh*, Tallabila Press, 1939.
'Into ethereal meads' from *This Vital Flesh*, Tallabila Press, 1939.
'Sextains' (two poems) from *Sextains*, Tallabila Press, 1939.

Mary Gilmore:

'Dedicatory' from *Selected Verse*, Angus & Robertson, 1948.
'Of Wonder' from *Selected Verse*, Angus & Robertson, 1948.
'Boolee, the Bringer of Life' from *Selected Verse*, Angus & Robertson, 1948.
'The Myall in Prison' from *Selected Verse*, Angus & Robertson, 1948.
'The Waradgery Tribe' from *Selected Verse*, Angus & Robertson, 1948.
'The Baying Hounds' from *Selected Verse*, Angus & Robertson, 1948.
'Nationality' from *Fourteen Men*, Angus & Robertson, 1954.
'The Dice were Loaded' from *Selected Verse*, Angus & Robertson, 1948.
'The Tenancy' from *Selected Verse*, Angus & Robertson, 1948.

Mary Fullerton:

'A Dream' from *Moles Do So Little with Their Privacy*, Angus & Robertson, 1942.
'Independence' from *Moles Do So Little with Their Privacy*, Angus & Robertson, 1942.
'Passivity' from *Moles Do So Little with Their Privacy*, Angus & Robertson, 1942.
'Lovers' from *Moles Do So Little with Their Privacy*, Angus & Robertson, 1942.
'Unit' from *Moles Do So Little with Their Privacy*, Angus & Robertson, 1942.
'Adventure' from *Moles Do So Little with Their Privacy*, Angus & Robertson, 1942.

Roderic Quinn:

'The Fisher' from *Poems*, Angus & Robertson, 1920.

James Devaney:

'Mortality' from *Poems*, Angus & Robertson, 1950.
'Winter Westerlies' from *Poems*, Angus & Robertson, 1950.

Hugh McCrae:

'Colombine' from *Colombine*, Angus & Robertson, 1920.
'June Morning' from *Colombine*, Angus & Robertson, 1920.
'Enigma' from *Colombine*, Angus & Robertson, 1920.
'Song of the Rain' from *Colombine*, Angus & Robertson, 1920.
'Ambuscade' from *Satyrs and Sunlight*, Fanfrolico Press, 1928.
'Morning' from *Satyrs and Sunlight*, Fanfrolico Press, 1928.
'The End of Desire' from *Satyrs and Sunlight*, Fanfrolico Press, 1928.
'Fragment' from *Australian Poetry*, Angus & Robertson, 1944.

Leonard Mann:
'The Earth' from *Poems from the Mask*, Hawthorn Press, 1951.
'Meditation in Winter' from *The Delectable Mountains*, Angus & Robertson, 1944.

E. G. Moll:
'Beware the Cuckoo' from *Beware the Cuckoo*, Australasian Publishing Co., 1947.
'On Having Grown Old' from *The Lifted Spear*, Angus & Robertson, 1953.

Kenneth Slessor:
'Earth-Visitors' from *One Hundred Poems*, Angus & Robertson, 1944.
'Stars' from *One Hundred Poems*, Angus & Robertson, 1944.
'Five Visions of Captain Cook' from *One Hundred Poems*, Angus & Robertson 1944.
'Crow Country' from *One Hundred Poems*, Angus & Robertson, 1944.
'Gulliver' from *One Hundred Poems*, Angus & Robertson, 1944.
'Sleep' from *One Hundred Poems*, Angus & Robertson, 1944.
'Five Bells' from *One Hundred Poems*, Angus & Robertson, 1944.
'Beach Burial' from *Australian Poetry*, Angus & Robertson, 1944.

John Thompson:
'Letter to a Friend' from *Thirty Poems*, Edwards & Shaw, 1954.

R. D. Fitzgerald:
'The cock that crowed this dawn up' from *Moonlight Acre*, Melbourne University Press, 1938.
'Essay on Memory' from *Moonlight Acre*, Melbourne University Press, 1938.
'1918–1941' from *This Night's Orbit*, Melbourne University Press, 1953.
'The Face of the Waters' from *This Night's Orbit*, Melbourne University Press, 1953.
'Traditional Tune' from *This Night's Orbit*, Melbourne University Press, 1953.

J. A. R. McKellar:
'Twelve O'Clock Boat' from *Collected Poems*, Angus & Robertson, 1946.

Ethel Anderson:
'Migrants' from *Australian Poetry*, Angus & Robertson, 1949.

Peter Hopegood:
    'Free Martin' from *Thirteen from Oahu*, Frank Johnson, 1940.
    'Dithyramb in Retrospect' from *Circus at World's End*, Angus & Robertson, 1947.

Max Dunn:
    'Flower of Exile' from *Time of Arrival*, privately printed.
    'I Danced Before I Had Two Feet' from *Australia Writes*, Cheshire, 1953.

Francis Brabazon:
    'Victoria Market' from *Early Poems*, Beacon Hill Publishing Co., 1953.

Brian Vrepont:
    'Net-menders' from *Beyond the Claw*, Angus & Robertson, 1952.
    'The Bomber' from *Australian Poetry*, Angus & Robertson, 1946.

A. D. Hope:
    'Australia' from *Meanjin*.
    'Standardization' from *Jindyworobak Anthology*, 1943.

Ronald McCuaig:
    'Betty by the Sea' from *Quod Ronald McCuaig*, Angus & Robertson, 1946.
    'Love Me and Never Leave Me' from *Quod Ronald McCuaig*, Angus & Robertson, 1946.
    'Is Love Not Everlasting?' from *Quod Ronald McCuaig*, Angus & Robertson, 1946.
    'The Daily Round' from *Quod Ronald McCuaig*, Angus & Robertson, 1946.

James Picot:
    'To the Rosella in the Poinsettia Tree' from *With a Hawk's Quill*, Meanjin Press, 1954.
    'Do You Not Hear' from *With a Hawk's Quill*, Meanjin Press, 1954.
    'Finale' from *With a Hawk's Quill*, Meanjin Press, 1954.

Ian Mudie:
    'Underground' from *Poems 1934–1944*, Georgian House, 1945.

Rex Ingamells:
    'Sea-chronicles' from *Australian Poetry*, Angus & Robertson, 1947.

William Hart-Smith:

'When You Touch' from *Harvest*, Jindyworobak Press, 1943.
'Drama' from *Jindyworobak Anthology*, 1943.
'Baiamai's Never-failing Stream' from *Harvest*, Jindyworobak Press, 1943.
'Columbus Goes West' from *Christopher Columbus*, Caxton Press, 1948.
'Bathymeter' from the *Bulletin*.

Roland Robinson:

'Casuarina' from *Language of the Sand*, Lyre-bird Writers, 1949.
'I Breathed into the Ash' from *Tumult of the Swans*, Lyre-bird Writers, 1953.
'The Rock-lily's Pale Spray' from *Tumult of the Swans*, Lyre-bird Writers, 1953.

Elizabeth Riddell:

'News of a Baby' from *Poems*, Ure Smith, 1948.
'Country Tune' from *Australian Poetry*, Angus & Robertson, 1953.
'Forebears' from *Australian Poetry*, Angus & Robertson, 1951–2.

Ken Barratt:

'Burke and Wills' from *Australian Poetry*, Angus & Robertson, 1946.

John Quinn:

'A Foxhole for the Night' from *Australian Poetry*, Angus & Robertson, 1945.

Douglas Stewart:

'Old Iron' from *The Dosser in Springtime*, Angus & Robertson, 1946.
'Terra Australis' from *Sun Orchids*, Angus & Robertson, 1952.
'The Sunflowers' from *Sun Orchids*, Angus & Robertson, 1952.
'Helmet Orchid' from *Sun Orchids*, Angus & Robertson, 1952.

Eve Langley:

'Native-born' from the *Bulletin*.
'Australia' from the *Bulletin*.
'This Year, Before It Ends' from the *Bulletin*.

Kenneth Mackenzie:

'Confession' from *The Moonlit Doorway*, Angus & Robertson, 1944.
'Caesura' from the *Bulletin*.
'The Snake' from *Australia Writes*, Cheshire, 1953.
'Legerdemain' from *Australian Poetry*, Angus & Robertson, 1951–2.

John Blight:
    'Becalmed' from *The Two Suns Met*, Lyre-bird Writers, 1954.
    'The Cat-o'-Nine-Tails' from *The Two Suns Met*, Lyre-bird Writers, 1954.
    'Crab' from the *Bulletin*.
    'Stonefish and Starfish' from the *Bulletin*.

Harold Stewart:
    'Dialogue of the Way' from *Meanjin*.

J. P. McAuley:
    'The Blue Horses' from *Under Aldebaran*, Melbourne University Press, 1947.
    'New Guinea Lament' from *Under Aldebaran*, Melbourne University Press, 1947.
    'Missa Papae Marcelli' from *Under Aldebaran*, Melbourne University Press, 1947.
    'The Death of Chiron' from *Australian Poetry*, Angus & Robertson, 1949–50.

Eric Irvin:
    'Midnight Patrol' from *Australian Poetry*, Angus & Robertson, 1944.
    'Brother Ass' from *Australian Poetry*, Angus & Robertson, 1947.
    'Christmas 1942' from *A Soldier's Miscellany*, Angus & Robertson, 1945.

Edgar Holt:
    'Two Sonnets from a Sequence' from *Meanjin*.

J. S. Manifold:
    'Fife Tune' from *Selected Verse*, Dennis Dobson, 1948.
    'Suburban Lullaby' from *Selected Verse*, Dennis Dobson, 1948.
    'The Tomb of Lt John Learmonth, A.I.F.' from *Selected Verse*, Dennis Dobson, 1948.

Judith Wright:
    'The Company of Lovers' from *The Moving Image*, Meanjin Press, 1946.
    'Bullocky' from *The Moving Image*, Meanjin Press, 1946.
    'Woman to Man' from *Woman to Man*, Angus & Robertson, 1949.
    'Woman's Song' from *Woman to Man*, Angus & Robertson, 1949.
    'Legend' from *The Gateway*, Angus & Robertson, 1953.
    'The Ancestors' from *The Gateway*, Angus & Robertson, 1953.
    'To a Child' from *The Gateway*, Angus & Robertson, 1953.

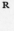

David Campbell:
    'Soldier's Song' from *Speak with the Sun*, Chatto & Windus, 1949.
    'Men in Green' from *Speak with the Sun*, Chatto & Windus, 1949.
    'Night Sowing' from the *Bulletin*.
    'Heart of Light' from the *Bulletin*.
    'The Monaro' from the *Bulletin*.
    'Beach Queen' from the *Bulletin*.

Val Vallis:
    'For This, the Tide' from the *Bulletin*.

Rosemary Dobson:
    'The Missal' from the *Bulletin*.
    'In My End is My Beginning' from *The Ship of Ice*, Angus & Robertson, 1948.
    'The Devil and the Angel (1)' from *The Ship of Ice*, Angus & Robertson, 1948
    'The Devil and the Angel (6)' from *The Ship of Ice*, Angus & Robertson, 1948.

Nan McDonald:
    'Wet Summer: Botanic Gardens' from the *Bulletin*.

Nancy Keesing:
    'Old Men' from *Imminent Summer*, Lyre-bird Writers, 1951.

David Rowbotham:
    'Little White Fox' from the *Bulletin*.
    'The Moment' from *Ploughman and Poet*, Lyre-bird Writers, 1954.

John Henderson:
    'Of Love and Time' from the *Bulletin*.

Mary Finnin:
    'Sarah Lorton' from the *Bulletin*.
    'Three Trees at Solstice' from the *Bulletin*.

Max Harris:
    'Lullaby' from *Angry Penguins*.
    'The Plowman' from *Angry Penguins*.
    'Martin Buber in the Pub' from *Direction*.

Geoffrey Dutton:
    'Nightflight and Sunrise' from *Nightflight and Sunrise*, Reed & Harris, 1944.
    'A Prisoner Freed' from *Australian Poetry*, Angus & Robertson, 1944.

Patricia Excell:
  'Forgotten Objects on a Beach' from *Meanjin*.
Francis Webb:
  'For My Grandfather' from *Leichhardt in Theatre*, Angus & Robertson, 1952.
  'The Gunner' from *Leichhardt in Theatre*, Angus & Robertson, 1952.
  'Laid-Off' from *Birthday*, privately printed.
  'Morgan's Country' from *Leichhardt in Theatre*, Angus & Robertson, 1952.
  'Cartier at St Malo' from *Leichhardt in Theatre*, Angus & Robertson, 1952.
Vincent Buckley:
  'Korea' from *Australia Writes*, Cheshire, 1953.
Charles Osborne:
  'So Fly by Night' from *Ern Malley's Journal*.
John Philip:
  'The Subject of the Bishop's Miracle' from *Australian Poetry*, Angus & Robertson, 1948.
Hal Porter:
  'Bi-focal' from the *Bulletin*.
Barrie Reid:
  'St Kilda' from *Ern Malley's Journal*.
  'Nothing' from *Ern Malley's Journal*.
Ray Mathew:
  'Young Man's Fancy' from *Australia Writes*, Cheshire, 1953
  'Let us not Pretend' from *With Cypress Pine*, Lyre-bird Writers, 1951.
  'Picnic' from the *Bulletin*.
  'The Poems come Easier' from *With Cypress Pine*, Lyre-bird Writers, 1951.

INDEX OF AUTHORS AND TITLES

(Note: For the purpose of this index authors are included under their own names, where they have used a pseudonym for writing purposes.)

257

INDEX OF AUTHORS AND TITLES

INDEX OF FIRST LINES

PRINTED IN GREAT BRITAIN BY
RICHARD CLAY AND COMPANY, LTD.,
BUNGAY, SUFFOLK.